Contents

Contents

Contents

Conducting E-commerce

by Loël McPhee & Peri Drucker

with Robert Cormia & Cathy Hammer

Inc. Business Resources
Boston, Massachusetts

Published by *Inc.* Business Resources,
a division of Gruner + Jahr USA Publishing,
publisher of *Inc.* magazine.
Copyright © 2000 by Gruner + Jahr USA Publishing,
Boston, MA
All rights reserved.

Book Project Manager: Gail E. Anderson
Text Designer: Martha Abdella
Editorial Director: Bradford W. Ketchum, Jr.

This publication is designed to provide accurate and
authoritative information in regard to the subject matter
covered. However, the publisher is not engaged in rendering
legal, accounting, or other professional advice. If legal
advice or other expert assistance is required, the services
of a competent professional should be sought. Companies that
conduct e-commerce on the Internet are evolving constantly,
as are URLs. While every effort has been made to ensure the
accuracy of information in this book, readers should be aware
that Web addresses are subject to change.

This book may be purchased in bulk at discounted rates for
sales promotions, premiums, or fund-raising. Custom books
and excerpts of this publication are available. Contact:
Custom Publishing Sales Dept.,
Inc. Business Resources, 38 Commercial Wharf,
Boston, MA 02110-3883 (1-800-394-1746).

Author Loël McPhee is a principal in Andiron Technologies.
She and author Peri Drucker are former employees of CommerceNet.
Andiron and CommerceNet are included in this book not for
promotional purposes, but rather, to illustrate certain
management practices.

ISBN 1-58230-015-1

First Edition

Printed in the United States of America.

www.inc.com

Chapter 1

Introduction to E-commerce

There is good reason why e-commerce is the topic of so many conversations and articles. It is not a fad. It is the future of selling. The sooner you get your company involved in it, the better edge you'll have in this increasingly competitive game.

You are probably familiar with the Internet and may already have registered your Web address, also known as a uniform resource locator, or URL (www.yourcompanyname.com). You may even have a marketing, or "brochureware," site, a noninteractive site that simply presents information just as a paper brochure would. (If you don't have your URL yet, now is the time to run, not walk, to your service provider to register your company.) You probably also know that you need to incorporate e-commerce into your business model, but you have a business to run and don't have the time to become an e-commerce expert. This book will help you get up to speed quickly.

What is e-commerce? In simplest terms, e-commerce means transacting business (buying and selling) over the Web. In a broader sense, e-commerce encompasses everything from how your customers find you to communicating with your customers and suppliers to the complete purchasing and delivery process. With the Internet and e-commerce, you can now do more business in less time and for less money than ever before. E-commerce is about expanding into new markets and sales channels as much as it's about improved service and enhanced business practices. Whether you conduct business-to-consumer (B2C) or business-to-business (B2B) e-commerce, it's all about making systems efficient and expanding market potential.

Like it or not, business is undergoing a revolution. New business models are emerging daily. New companies have appeared that have changed consumers' buying behavior forever. Look at what Amazon.com has done to the book-selling business. It's successfully competing against well-established, high-end bookstores as well as discount chains.

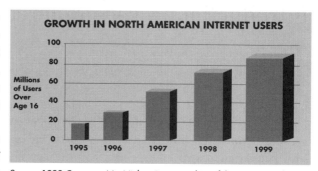

GROWTH IN NORTH AMERICAN INTERNET USERS

Source: 1999 CommerceNet Nielsen Demographics of the Internet Study

Having a Web site is just the tip of the iceberg. How your Web site interacts with your customers and functions within your business is the heart of e-commerce. E-commerce has brought about solutions that integrate data, applications, and processes that allow your customers to easily find product information, place and track orders online, and communicate with you.

Throughout this book you will find case studies of businesses that have made the most of e-commerce. And at the end of each chapter you will find their URLs so you can check out their Web sites yourself. wine.com is an example of a company that considers the customer every step of the way. It is an interesting, informative, and well-designed site that appeals to all levels of wine expertise, from the casual wine drinker to the aficionado. wine.com's interface includes easy-to-understand categories and detailed searching methods. All transactions are conducted with superior security in place. Special features include an inexpensive wine club that entitles its members to monthly delivery of wine and educational materials.

More than just a retail site, wine.com has created a community of people with a common interest. It offers a free newsletter that features news, information on special wines, tips from the team, and discounts. It adds even further excitement by offering a contest to win a free trip to wine country. It is no wonder that it continuously adds to its database of potential customers.

In the following chapters you will be given guidance in building a first-class site like wine.com. The fast-paced evolution of e-commerce can be used to your benefit. While there may always be something bigger and better on the horizon, don't let that stop you from getting started now. Begin planning and implementing your e-commerce site today. Just make sure it's flexible and open so that it can change and adapt as new technology is introduced. That way, your site will continue to grow and be better and easier to use.

Who's using the Internet, and who's buying? CommerceNet, a global e-commerce consortium, and Nielsen Media Research have surveyed the usage and purchasing patterns of the North American population since 1995 (see chart on opposite page). At that time, 10% of the population over the age of 16 had accessed the Internet. Now almost 50% of the population over the age of 16 is online. April 1999 showed 92 million people on the Internet; 60% of them shopped online and 28 million of them (about 30%) made a purchase online. This rate of increase is expected to continue until about 75% of the population is online.

Not only are more people online, they're spending more time and more money there. The table on the left shows the average monthly expenditures of people shopping online.

Early sales over the Internet were pri-

AVERAGE ONLINE EXPENDITURES	
Amount (monthly)	% online shoppers
Less than $10	28.8%
$10 to less than $100	48.3%
$100 to less than $200	11.4%
$200 to less than $300	4.1%
$300 to less than $400	0.7%
$400 to less than $500	1.1%
$500 or more	4.1%
Don't know	1.4%
Refuse to say	0.1%

Source: 1999 CommerceNet Nielsen Demographics of the Internet Study

marily of computer hardware and software. The majority of the online population comprised males in the computer industry, so the products offered reflected that. As a wider variety of people, from teenagers to working women to senior citizens, got "hooked up," vendors followed. Now cars, books, and clothing are among the most popular items sold on the Web. Selling on the Internet is not only possible, it can be extremely profitable.

Online retailing to consumers isn't the only business model thriving on the Web. Business-to-business ventures, in which companies interact with their suppliers and vendors, are using the Internet to communicate and do business more efficiently with their supply-chain partners. The forecast for growth through 2003 appears below.

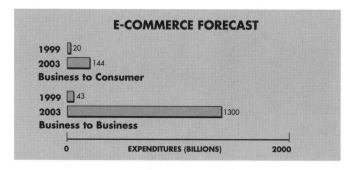

Source: Forrester Research

A consumer-driven economy. The Internet is moving our economy from an industry-driven model to a consumer-driven model. As consumers interact more with online companies, major changes in products and services and in the way they are presented to consumers will be apparent. In the old model, consumers received advertising messages and were persuaded to buy what was available. In the new consumer-driven economy, shoppers have more choice and will demand products and services that suit their needs. E-commerce is the beginning of this change.

E-commerce is no longer an alternative; it's an imperative. Consumers today shop and compare a great deal more than they did in the past, and the Internet gives them an amazingly powerful tool to do so. Operating a Web site, particularly an e-commerce–enabled site, is becoming increasingly critical in today's market.

For companies that manage the game skillfully, e-commerce will bring growth and revenue. For others, e-commerce will enable them to simply stay in business. Dan Williams, an independent retailer, saw the writing on the wall three years ago, when his family-owned power-tool and plumbing-supplies company, Louis Williams & Sons, in Hendersonville, N.C., began losing market share to the giant chains. With co-op advertising dollars from tool manufacturer Makita, Williams developed a Web site. Although Williams had lost 20% of his retail sales to the chains, that revenue has been replaced by his Internet and catalog sales. "Going online didn't increase our revenue; it was a revenue shift," Williams explains. "It's kept us alive."

If your customers aren't already buying online, they will be over the next couple of years, and they will expect to find you on the Internet. If you aren't there, they may well go elsewhere. ■

**COMPANIES AND SITES
IN THIS CHAPTER**

Amazon.com **www.amazon.com**
CommerceNet **www.commerce.net**
Louis Williams & Sons
www.makita-direct.com
Nielsen Media Research
www.nielsenmedia.com
wine.com **www.wine.com**

Chapter 2

Are You Ready for E-commerce?

Are You Ready?

ZOOTS is a Newton, Mass., dry cleaning and laundry-services company with an Internet twist. Founded in 1998 by the creators of the Staples office-supply chain, Tom Stemberg and Todd Krasnow, ZOOTS offers traditional dry cleaning and laundry services with the addition of e-mail order-ready notification and pick-up reminders, plus promotional coupons delivered via the Internet. It's quick and easy to sign up online and list your preference for starch and for having shirts hung, not folded.

ZOOTS is an excellent example of the new "clicks-and-mortar" business model. A clicks-and-mortar company combines its existing real-world business with the best of online business. By taking its traditional "bricks and mortar" service company and adding mouse-click ease to enhance the customer experience, ZOOTS has seen its business grow.

Why adding e-commerce is a big step. Is your business ready to expand into e-commerce? Let's assume you have already posted a brochureware Web site that announces your existence and markets your services or products. Now you want to enable customers to make purchases and place orders on your site. Integrating this kind of transactional capability into your site is a big step.

You'll need to decide which level of e-commerce best suits your company. Even starting e-commerce at a basic level can enhance your current operations. At first, it may be a challenge to balance ongoing business with the new workflow process of an e-commerce site. The best approach may be to develop a clicks-and-mortar Web presence that enhances your current transactions, rather than build a Web store and treat it as a separate entity in your company's business model.

As you expand your e-commerce capabilities, you should also keep reviewing your entire business plan. Remember, e-commerce isn't just about selling online; it's also about making your business more efficient. But planning, designing, and implementing a Web store is an investment of both time and money. It's worth developing a plan for your new hybrid business model and exploring all your options thoroughly.

When ZOOTS moved into e-commerce, it used the Internet to expand the traditional dry-cleaning business model. While it offers the convenience of online scheduling and payment and other options, it continues to support its retail locations and those customers who don't want to use an Internet-based service.

Ways your company might integrate a clicks-and-mortar strategy include allowing product purchases online, with customer pick-up at physical locations; constructing a return policy that gives the customer the option of going to a retail store; and offering alternative delivery methods that can be tracked through the site. The goal is to maximize the customer experience, not decrease options.

The cost of developing a site. The actual costs of designing and implementing a transactional Web storefront, without taking into consideration any software and hardware upgrades and changes, can range from nothing to several thousand dollars. (In fact, big companies often spend hundreds of thousands of dollars.) The "free" solution involves only the cost of your time and your merchant account for a simple, template-based Web site hosted on an e-commerce–enabled service provider. However, the average initial setup cost for an e-commerce–enabled Web site for small to midsize businesses ranges from $500 to $15,000, with monthly costs ranging from $100 to $5,000. The actual cost will be determined by several factors.

1. Intricacy of the design, including graphics and functionality

2. Variety of functional elements used on the site, such as:

- A shopping cart (a sophisticated technology that allows a person to shop and store products in a "cart" for "checkout" later)
- Search capabilities
- Customization that allows the shopper to personalize the buying experience
- Feedback systems for interaction with customers

3. *Size of the site, including:*
- Number of products offered
- Amount of information provided

4. *Additions to your existing business, such as:*
- Rented or purchased infrastructure
- New and outsourced personnel
- Marketing launch
- Shipping or delivery options, and other subcontracts

5. *Ongoing costs, including:*
- Amount and frequency of site maintenance
- Adding or changing products offered through the site
- Site redesign as required
- Personnel costs
- Ongoing marketing costs

The following seven strategies will help you plan a successful launch of your e-commerce Web site:

1. Conduct market research on your customers and competition. How ready are your existing customers to buy online? Evaluate your customer base. Are they already using the Internet? Are they making purchases over the Web? Are they part of a demographic group that is likely to find shopping on the Web an exciting option? Although the Internet is capable of expanding your customer base globally, it is most likely that new customers will initially share many characteristics of your current customers. So answering these questions will tell you if your investment is likely to pay off.

Then ask whether your competition is conducting e-commerce. How many of your competitors have a Web presence? How many sell online? What virtual competitors are entering your market?

Survey the companies you consider your competition. Then log on and try out their Web sites. You can download a form to fill out as you evaluate each site, from the Web site of *Inc.* magazine. Go to www.inc.com/freetools/1,7182,CHL9,00.html. Then search the Free Tool listing for "Web Site Evaluation Worksheet." Once you have rated each site it helps to draw a matrix showing your competitors and the things they are doing. Ask yourself how you can improve on what they are doing or in what new ways you can serve the customers.

Next, check to see if there are any new Internet-only companies in your market space. Engage in some practical research. Do a search to find one or more Web sites that provide a similar product or service to yours. If possible, go through the entire process of making a purchase. Is the competition's site hard to use? Do your competitors guarantee security? Do they have the same selection of goods? What are their delivery and return policies like? Hands-on experience is invaluable.

John Wooster, owner of the Bon Air Health store, in Greenbrae, Calif., is planning to post a Web site, and he's approaching the project the right way. Wooster analyzed his competition by going to popular health sites, such as PlanetRx.com, drugstore.com, and MotherNature.com, and looked through broader health listings on America Online (AOL) and AltaVista. He found ways he hadn't thought of to attract new customers. He will add value to his current services by posting specials on his future Web site and by sending e-mail notifications. He sees a niche his competition has left open, and he plans to fill it.

2. Define your value position. How well does your product or service lend itself to Web purchase or interaction? Will a Web presence add value for your customers? Can your current customers use a Web site to reorder goods and services? Is it enough to develop a Web site that makes the shopping experience easier for your existing customers? Others may have thought of new ways to approach a business similar to yours. Look at those sites for ideas.

Ask yourself, "How will I differentiate my business from that of my competition?" This is a key question. After all, how many Web sites selling socks does one world need? Start with what you probably already know—that is, what distinguishes your business from your real-world competitors right now. Can you afford to compete on price? Is your physical location and resulting low shipping costs to local customers a plus? Is your selection unique? What similar inventory from competitors is currently available online?

Differentiation can be created in two areas: differentiation between what you can offer online as opposed to what you offer in a bricks-and-mortar store, and differentiation in the shopping experience for the customer. Either type of differentiation is a valid reason to develop a Web presence.

The online arm of the famous Lands' End has developed an extremely successful Web site. One thing that differentiates landsend.com from many of its online and paper-catalog competitors is "The Overstocks Store" feature. Overstocks are offered at an additional discount that increases as the items remain unsold. The site includes a listing that displays the original price and the amount of the price reduction. New items are listed every Wednesday and Saturday. Landsend.com also sends e-mails at customized intervals that inform registered shoppers when items are offered at discounted prices.

3. Get buy-in from all employees. Is the Web perceived as a natural next step for your business, or are you the only visionary in your company? A successful e-commerce implementation needs to have buy-in from your entire workforce, from upper management down through the ranks. It's worth taking the time and effort to provide clear explanations of the process, from planning to maintenance, to your entire staff. This is a big decision and will probably cause a cultural shift in your organization, so it's best to get everyone on board. It's particularly crucial that anyone within your organization who deals with customers is supportive of your new e-commerce strategy. They might know things about your customers or daily workflow that could improve the development of your site. Involving and/or promoting your new Web venture to everyone within your company, therefore, will help your efforts in the long run.

4. Assess the impact of your new online sales channel. Will online sales compete with your current sales channels? This is an important issue. There are many cases of companies that charged in to join the e-commerce

TIP If you currently sell directly to the end user, then an e-commerce site is a natural extension of your direct sales. If, however, you sell through distributors and/or retailers, it is wise not to undermine the business, but instead to develop incentives that invite their cooperation. Consider profiling on your site retailers that carry your product. Or better yet, offer a rebate for local sales.

revolution and ended up alienating their current sales channels.

Talk your plans through with your business partners to determine if you will have channel conflicts. If so, work with them from the start to find a resolution. You want them to be supporters of your new Web endeavor, not to see it as a threat.

Andiron Technologies, a company that makes a pollution-reducing device for open fireplaces, came up with a unique plan. While the company normally sells directly to the user, it didn't want to alienate mom-and-pop stores that sell hearth products. Andiron realized potential customers were likely to ask about its product at these small retailers, so it wanted to develop a good relationship with them. The company decided to let retailers order the product from the Andiron Web site and have it shipped directly to the customer. This way, the retailer makes a commission on a product it might not otherwise carry, without shelling out any of the associated costs of keeping the product on hand. Furthermore, customers perceive the retailers as very up-to-date about using the Internet to save them time and money.

Bob Duncan is a business owner who learned the hard way that Web-based sales need to be developed properly. His nine-year-old company, American Leather, based in Dallas, Tex., manufactures 80 different collections of custom leather furniture, which were sold through select higher-end retail dealers throughout the country. Typical of the furniture industry, American Leather provided each dealer with exclusive rights to specific collections within a given market area. When the same merchandise became available online, however, dealers several states away were able to sell the same inventory at highly competitive prices.

Duncan began getting complaints from his most important dealers. He responded by creating an Internet policy that prohibited dealers from promoting the American Leather brand on their individual Web sites. But Duncan soon realized he was literally telling his dealers they couldn't promote American Leather's brand over the fastest growing, most revolutionary information medium in the world. Clearly, he needed another solution.

Adapting to the new medium, Duncan redesigned American Leather's own site to include more-detailed product information and an automated "dealer locator." Duncan still prohibits dealers from selling American Leather products on their individual Web sites. His new Web strategy, however, gives customers added service while protecting his dealers from unnecessary competition—an arrangement the dealers are happy with.

TIP Another aspect of introducing a Web-based sales channel is the impact it might have on customers. Make sure you're increasing their choices of ways to do business with you, not making things more complicated. Some retailers have gotten into trouble by offering merchandise on their sites that has no connection to their retail outlets or by requiring that certain items be returned only through the site. This can complicate the customer's shopping experience and make your company less, not more, attractive to buy from.

5. Profile your typical customer. Do you know who your customers are and how they conduct their shopping? Online, you don't get the same face-to-face feedback you get in person, but there are still ways of personalizing the customer experience. Understanding the demographics (gender, age, wage) and psychographics (lifestyle) of your typical customer is essential for determining the best way to set up your site. It is also crucial to have a thorough understanding of the entire shopping process. You should know how customer selections are made, how the order is placed, what the expectations are for service and delivery, what customer support is required, and so forth.

The Web site can enhance, and even replace, the physical shopping experience. However, it is most likely to be successful if the design is based on what you know about how your customers like to shop and then builds from there. What are the items people usually like to see right away? What questions do they typically ask about your inventory or service? Put these things up front on your site the same way you'd put them up front in your store. To approach the design of your transactional Web site without this knowledge is foolish, and the design is likely to fail.

If you have a physical business, you're probably well aware of the profile of your typical customer. If not, start by calling your customers and asking them a few simple questions. Or you may decide to enclose a customer survey with your product. When Andiron Technologies started out, free delivery was standard for units that were sold within its vicinity. Having delivery people in their homes encouraged customers to fill out product-survey forms. Through this feedback, the company learned that its customers, while pleased with reducing pollution, were equally impressed by the ease of lighting a fire with the product. Andiron adapted its marketing strategy accordingly, and placed these testimonials on the home page.

6. Make contingency plans for rapid growth. Can you handle a major success? Although not all e-commerce offerings are immediate hits, instant success does happen. You have all heard stories about the companies that are making it big. Managing explosive growth is a real issue in the world of e-commerce. Can you handle a 10-fold increase in customer calls and e-mails? Can you bring on additional personnel to manage customer support? How long will it take to get them up to speed? What if you have 100-fold the number of inquiries? Are you prepared to outsource your customer service? How would you find this resource? Do you have enough documentation to get an outside vendor up to speed within a limited time frame? What about inventory and fulfillment?

Success can be as detrimental as failure if you don't adequately plan for it. You probably remember Christmas 1999, when several toy sites could not fulfill their online orders. Being unprepared can seriously damage your company's reputation. If you haven't prepared for big success, you may want to start out on a smaller scale. Several small-scale options are mentioned in Chapter 3. You may also want to build your e-commerce site but market it slowly. Once you have outlined your plans for growth and are prepared—go for it!

Consider the example of the online wine seller, wine.com, which entered the 1999 holiday season prepared—or so Tim Moran, senior vice-president of operations, and the managers thought. The managers boosted their customer-service department 20-fold to handle the overflow of new-customer calls they expected. But the volume was beyond expectations. Fortunately, they had hired a great team of people, who worked around the clock, managed the volume, and prevented wine.com from ending up profiled in the press as one of the retailers unable to keep up with the high holiday demand.

7. Assess your internal resources. What new roles might you have to fill when you move to e-commerce? Determine the scope of the project and the resources you have to handle it internally. Clearly write out job descriptions, responsibilities, and time frames. Understanding your resources and assessing your core competencies is the first step in deciding how much to keep in-house and how much to outsource. Even if you outsource most of the work, you will still need to delegate responsibilities for updating and working with your e-commerce vendors.The responsibilities that must be addressed include:

- Developing the scope and design of the Web site
- Writing Web-site copy, including descriptions of products or services
- Posting changes and additions to the Web site
- Hardware selection and maintenance
- Software selection and maintenance
- Customer service and support
- Tracking and analyzing Web-site performance

This list does not include the additional resources you might need for the e-commerce efforts you probably already use in the normal course of your business, including:

- Marketing and promotions
- Buying
- Mail room
- Operations
- Finance and accounting

Adopting e-commerce: The push from businesses and consumers. Sooner or later, companies will be forced to adopt e-commerce to stay current and competitive. Elements that will cause this transformation are basic business concerns: suppliers, competitors, and customers.

As more companies adopt e-commerce, they will require their business partners to also transact business electronically. Virtually every large company has already begun to implement some sort of e-commerce. For a large company, the savings that electronic procurement systems generate through reduced errors, time and man-hour savings, and standardization are significant. These larger companies are, in turn, requiring their trading partners to implement compatible e-commerce systems to allow them to share information and services electronically. As smaller companies implement those systems, they are sure to benefit as well.

Companies that can offer a variety of services to both consumers and other businesses through their Web sites will have the competitive edge. Given a choice of suppliers with relatively similar products, any company that has already shifted to electronic business transactions will ultimately choose trading partners who also conduct their business over the Web.

OpenTable.com, based in San Francisco, Calif., is an interesting hybrid of a business-to-consumer service with a business-to-business value proposition.

To the consumer, OpenTable provides a great new way to book and confirm reservations at top restaurants across the country. The OpenTable.com network enables users to search for available seating by cuisine type, neighborhood, price, or from a previously established list of favorite restaurants. Diners can confirm and cancel reservations from their computers at their convenience. They can also send digital dining invitations to guests. All these services are provided to diners free of charge.

From the business-to-business angle, OpenTable.com derives its revenue from the restaurants it serves on its network. It has developed a Web site that gives restaurateurs the ability to manage various resources, such as number of tables, employees, capacity planning, and a database of customers.

For the restaurateur, the "electronic reservation book" that connects to the Internet is not just a means of receiving reservations. It delivers all the flexibility and features of expensive back-office reservation-management software, capturing valuable management information. It organizes reservation sheets, seating charts, waiting lists, driving directions, and a customer database.

Customer demand. The push for businesses to get on board with e-commerce will also come from customers. One example of this phenomenon is the arrival of the common grocery store on the Web. Companies such as Webvan Group have created a value-added experience by allowing you to order your groceries online and have them delivered. As a customer, your initial reaction to online grocery shopping may be to question someone else's ability to select produce or fresh meat for you. But how much of the average shopping cart is filled with staples? Is it really necessary to touch a roll of paper towels? Even if shoppers insist on personally selecting their own produce, significant time and effort can be removed from the shopper's schedule. Lists can be standardized and customized through the Webvan site, making this errand as simple as clicking a few buttons.

How much will you save? E-commerce is not only about broadening your reach and market potential; it is also about efficiency. Web-based answers to frequently asked questions (FAQs) can save time and money answering repetitive inquiries about your products and services. From store and office locations to operation times, from product descriptions to your return policy and procedures, storing this information on the Internet will save you time. Automated shipping and tracking capabilities can also save time and money spent researching a customer's order status.

The nature of the Internet and the sheer volume of users can significantly reduce the cost and time of acquiring each new customer. In an example from Jaclyn Easton's book, *StrikingItRich.com: Profiles of 23 Incredibly Successful Websites You've Probably Never Heard Of* (McGraw-Hill Companies, 2000), Daniel Harrison of poolandspa.com had created a decent mail-order business with a list of 2,000 names that had taken him 17 years to collect. In his first year on the Web, Harrison accumulated 5,000 more names, and now poolandspa.com's repeat business from the Web exceeds 80%.

The automated nature of your Web site can reduce errors made by hand-entering orders. Sites can store customer information for duplicate or future orders. If your Web site is tied into your back-end systems, a real cost savings can be derived from the reduction of processes.

While cost savings and growth can be seen on the customer side of your Web site, the potential for real savings arises from the supply side of your business. As you bring your suppliers online, you will save time with online procurement, forecasting, and projections. Of course, this savings can be realized only if your Web site is completely integrated into your business. ■

COMPANIES AND SITES IN THIS CHAPTER

AltaVista **www.altavista.com**

America Online **www.aol.com**

American Leather **www.americanleather.com**

Andiron Technologies **www.ecofire.com**

Ask Jeeves **www.ask.com**

drugstore.com **www.drugstore.com**

Dogpile **www.dogpile.com**

MetaCrawler **www.metacrawler.com**

Hoover's Online: The Business Network **www.hoovers.com**

Iconocast **www.iconocast.com**

Inc. magazine **www.inc.com**

Lands' End **www.landsend.com**

MotherNature.com **www.mothernature.com**

OpenTable.com **www.opentable.com**

PlanetRx.com **www.planetrx.com**

poolandspa.com **www.poolandspa.com**

Webvan Group **www.webvan.com**

wine.com **www.wine.com**

ZOOTS **www.zoots.com**

Chapter 3

Testing the Waters

After you've gone through the seven strategies in Chapter 2, you may find that you're not quite ready to develop an e-commerce-enabled Web site for your company. If you simply want to test the waters first, there are some inexpensive ways you can try selling your products and services online.

This chapter shows you a few of these quick and easy alternatives, including placing online ads, selling your product or service through an online auction site, and profiling your services on a group purchasing site. These are great ways to expand your normal distribution channels using the Web, without spending a lot of money.

Classified Web ads. Certainly, one of the easiest ways to test the Web is to place an ad in the online classifieds. Many of these services are free and easy to use. For instance, Yahoo!, one of the most popular Web sites, allows you to select a category for your ad and use online forms to enter your ad information. Also, almost every newspaper has an online presence, with a classifieds section. You can use these electronic versions just as you would your local paper, but you get global coverage.

Online auctions. The best-known sales model for e-commerce is the online auction. Virtually no one predicted that eBay, for example, would be one of the biggest success stories of the Internet. But eBay is now the busiest and most well known online auction site, with more than four million items for sale. It has expanded into five other countries.

But eBay is by no means alone in the online auction market. By submitting the question "How can I learn about online auctions?" to the Ask Jeeves site recently, we received a list of 29 Web-based auctions. But that number underestimates the spread of auction sites. Back in 1998, a CNET article put the number of auction houses at that time at more than 150. The list has grown to include traditional auction houses, such as Sothebys, and large sites, such as Amazon.com, which have added auctioning components.

Commercial versus person-to-person auctions. There are two categories of online auctions. Commercial auctions are held by companies such as Egghead Onsale Auctions, which own the items or facilitate the auction of large quantities of goods. Person-to-person auctions, in which consumers contact sellers directly, take place on such sites as eBay. Despite the name, person-to-person auctions are not for individuals only. Many companies take advantage of these auctions, and the auction sites welcome them. Just check out Business Exchange on eBay. If you have a large quantity of goods that you want to sell in a lot, the commercial auction house is for you. You either contract to sell the items directly to the auction house and they take it from there, or you post the entire lot on the auction site and wait until it's sold.

An online auction allows sellers to post goods or services on a Web site, and buyers to enter bids to purchase the items. Online auctions are run identically to their real-world counterparts, except that bidders participate over the Internet rather than in person or on the phone. The seller has the option to set a minimum, or "reserve," price

TIP Kathleen Seiders, professor of marketing and entrepreneurship at Babson College, in Wellesley, Mass., suggests test marketers try selling the same product a few times at an auction site, but varying the opening bid, description, and pictures. "Online auctions can be a way to test which marketing messages are most effective and which prices get the best response," says Seiders. But she warns that such feedback is useless in a vacuum. "You need to benchmark your findings against what's considered solid demand at that site for the type of product you're trying to sell," she says.

below which he will not sell the item. There is a stated time limit in which all bids must be entered.

Market-test validity. Market testing via an online auction is most valid if the customers (the auction audience) are similar to your company's customers. The same type of people who read traditional print classified ads, for instance, tend to read online classifieds and auction listings. If your product is a familiar one, an auction may well be an appropriate way for you to test the online market.

Various online auctions handle the money and item exchanges differently. Some auctions merely bring the buyer and seller together, with the actual financial transactions and delivery details handled entirely by the parties involved. There are new services, such as PayPal, by X.com, whose business is to aid in the transfer of funds between individuals. Easy and quick to use, this service allows any user to pay or receive payment electronically. Other sites enable the financial transaction to take place over their sites and also arrange pick-up and delivery of the items.

TIP PayPal allows you to send money securely to any e-mail user in the United States. After signing up, you simply enter the recipient's e-mail address and a dollar amount. The money is charged to your credit card and sent to the recipient, who then registers and is immediately credited with the amount of money in the new account.

To find a listing of online auctions for a particular product, check out the Internet Auction List.

Don't get caught in the trap of thinking that online auctions are only for Beanie Babies and "garage sale" items. Companies auction services as well as products. (As an example, see the ad on the next page for the auction of a hotel stay.)

Innovative companies use auc-

Services, as well as products, can be auctioned online, as this posting proves.

tions as marketing tools, essentially replacing traditional contests and raffles. Gary Helland, a wedding photographer who specializes in photography anywhere in the country, offers his services to the winner of an online auction. Prior to his introduction to the Web, Gary's business, Helland Photographs of Phoenix, Ariz., was generated primarily by word of mouth. Now he gets 80% of his business through the Internet. Business quadrupled overnight when he put his site up and used simple techniques to promote his business. For example, a bride in Budapest, Hungary, who was planning to be married in San Francisco, recently contacted Gary after reading the online posting shown on the next page.

Group purchase sites and bartering. Another way to experiment with e-commerce is through group purchasing sites, such as Mercata and Mobshop. On these sites, buying is encouraged through the business model that lowers the price as the volume goes up. Consumers receive volume discounts by being part of a group of people who want to buy the same product. Interested buyers spread the word to their friends and family who might be interested in going in on the purchase, which drives the price down and increases the customer base. As in the auctions, a time limit is put on the purchase process. And again, the site handles the financial side of the transaction, with the seller handling the fulfillment and shipping end of the purchase.

Barter sites are another method of experimenting with e-commerce. Companies such as Internet Barter enable the exchange of goods and services through the age-old method. Bartering reduces your inventory while allowing you to receive goods and products your company needs, without the

CONGRATULATIONS ON YOUR UPCOMING WEDDING!

You are about to bid on the opportunity to work with and have your wedding photographed by one of the truly great wedding photographers in America. Photographing weddings from Los Angeles to New York, Gary Helland has created a new concept in world-class wedding photography for your special day. All aspects before, during, and after are captured in a style both dramatic and exciting. The winning bidder, getting married anywhere in America, will receive virtually unlimited coverage for up to TWO FULL DAYS. Everything is covered. Nothing is missed! For examples of Gary's extraordinary work, please view his Web site at www.hellandphoto.com. All potential bidders should contact Gary through his Web site prior to bidding to ensure his availability for your wedding date. You can also call Gary, toll free, at 1-888-777-0985. At that time, Gary will detail exactly what your package will include, payment terms, etc.

need for significant money to change hands.

Internet malls and partnerships with existing e-tailers. One of the most popular ways to test-run e-commerce is by listing your company with one of the online malls. Online malls display a number of Web stores all in one place, making it easier for the shopper to find a desired item. They also enable the shopper to search for an item in all the participating stores.

For the merchant, malls provide many advantages. Various malls conduct business differently. Some malls allow you to list individual items while others offer the opportunity to use their templates to create your own Web page, which is then hosted on their site.

Online malls use different models for the back end of the transaction. For example, Yahoo!'s "Yahoo! Store" handles the financial transactions for merchants by connecting directly to their merchant accounts. Amazon.com's zShops model acts as a middleman, taking the orders for merchants, who then contact their shoppers to complete the sales offline.

Malls also serve as important marketing vehicles. They can bring a higher profile to small businesses by including them with well-known sites, much the same way a Macy's or a Crate & Barrel can bring foot traffic to lesser-known shops in a physical mall. Some specialty malls share a theme, attracting shoppers looking for stores and products that fall into the same category. While they drive traffic to your site, most thematic malls require that you have a site of your own.

One last method of testing the Web using someone else's site is to ask other e-tailers to carry your product for you. As there are thousands of new Internet retailers, you can probably find a compatible company to promote and profile your products or services along with its own inventory.

Sites without financial transactions. One way many companies begin selling over the Internet is by operating a Web site that is limited to alerting them when someone wants to place an order with their company. These sites use various methods. One allows the customer to submit an order that generates an e-mail to the merchant. Another is a posted order form the customer prints out and faxes to the merchant. It is still up to the customer to submit credit-card information or send a check to complete the transaction.

The Web site of J. P. Faddoul Co., a 35-year-old giftware and bridal-registry shop in Shrewsbury, Mass., offers e-mail-based customer support and direction. For instance, visitors can submit their crystal, flatware, and/or china patterns in a special form, and Faddoul will e-mail a list of the available pieces in the requested pattern(s). Faddoul is a small business, operated by just three family members, so the shop does not have the resources to support transactional e-commerce. When a customer hits the "Order" button on the Faddoul Web site, a screen pops up directing the buyer to call the shop or send an e-mail inquiry, and the shop will call back to complete the transaction.

Carole Levene, the owner of Timeshare Resales USA, an Orlando-based brokerage that sells timeshares, has found that even though her customers don't complete their transactions online, the company still makes a lot of money with its Web site. Once a potential buyer finds something of interest at the site, he or she just clicks on the handy buyer's form, fills out the necessary information, and Timeshares makes the contact to close the deal. The Web accounts for 99% of Levene's revenues. However, as online shopping becomes more the standard among consumers, sites that don't allow instant purchasing will likely lose critical market share.

Where to go from here. All these options allow you to explore online selling. Once you've tested the waters of Internet-based sales, without developing an entire e-commerce-enabled Web site, you should be able to determine where you want to position your company online and what dollar investment you are willing to make. The next step is to go fully transactional. ■

COMPANIES AND SITES IN THIS CHAPTER

Amazon.com **www.amazon.com**

Ask Jeeves **www.ask.com**

CNET **www.cnet.com**

eBay **www.ebay.com**

Egghead.com **www.egghead.com**

Helland Photographs **www.hellandphoto.com**

Internet Auction List **www.internetauctionlist.com**

Internet Barter **www.bartertrust.com**

Mercata **www.mercata.com**

Mobshop **www.mobshop.com**

Sothebys **www.sothebys.com**

Stonewall Bed & Breakfast
www.swva.net/stonewall/stonewall.html

Timeshare Resales USA **www.timesharesusa.com**

X.com **www.paypal.com**

Yahoo! **www.yahoo.com**

Chapter 4

Outsource vs. In-house

T he first Web site posted by Andiron Technologies, a Woodside, Calif.-based environmental-solutions product development company, was designed by a friend and hosted on a friend of a friend's computer. It was a great way to start, but the site quickly got into trouble. It went down frequently, and response time to problems was slow. Then the site-designer friend became increasingly in demand for other projects and didn't have time to keep up with Andiron. Something had to change.

First, Andiron moved the site to a reputable Internet service provider (ISP). The site stayed up, and access to it improved. In addition, the ISP provided Andiron with valuable traffic and analysis tools.

But the site still wasn't quite working for them. Andiron's product line had grown from one item to four, making the original order system difficult to use. It was time to revamp the site. The owners had to decide whether to make the changes themselves with some of the available tools or to hire a professional developer. They chose a fairly cost-effective solution by doing most of the work in-house, but outsourcing the storefront to an e-commerce service provider.

Once you decide to incorporate e-commerce functionality into your company's Web site, the next decision is how to accomplish the task. You need to consider the design, creation, functionality, hosting, and maintenance of the Web site. Any of those can be handled internally or outsourced, and the choice is an important one.

Today many companies choose an e-commerce–enabled service provider that supplies a packaged solution, addressing all the needs in a one-stop shop.

As an alternative, various elements of the site can be created and hosted at different places. Firms create and host their Web sites by keeping Webstore software on one server and linking to an e-commerce application on a provider's server. Transparent to the user, these two systems connect with a single click.

Up front and back office. There are two layers to every e-commerce Web site: the "up front" and the "back office." Up front is composed of the components the customer uses (see Chapter 5). Back office is what happens behind the scenes once a purchase is made (see Chapter 6). Although these elements must appear coordinated and seamless to the user, in fact, they may be totally separate elements, with parts handled by different companies located anywhere in the world.

On a retail site, the product catalog can sit on one server that is easily accessed, while the e-commerce elements, such as ordering and payment processing, are kept on a secure server that has special software limiting access. So you could take care of the upkeep on your own copy and images while employing an outside company to handle the transactions.

You need to decide just how much of the control, responsibility, and resources of your site maintenance you want to take on. You can also choose how much you want to be involved in the creative and functional development of your Web store. Complete (or almost complete) control is important to some businesses, but this level of involvement can take time and attention away from running other areas of your business.

The following sections give you an overview of the current e-commerce landscape, including definitions, key providers, and costs associated with each solution. Because this is a rapidly changing arena, with new vendors and features constantly entering the scene, examples are provided for illustrative purposes and do not represent the full range of companies in each industry segment. Check out the Web for some of the most up-to-date listings, including reviews of vendors and services. inc.com is a great start, along with other industry sites, such as Tophost.com, ECnow.com, and CNET's Builder.com.

Who should host your Web site? When it comes to Web hosting, you have three options: hosting internally, co-locating, and outsourcing. Web-site hosts used to act only as a receptacle and server for the files that constituted the Web site. Today many hosting companies provide e-commerce functionality as well.

Hosting internally. Hosting internally means you own the server (a computer dedicated to exchanging information over the Internet with other computers) and that it is physically located in your place of business. It is crucial that the server be continually connected to the Internet 24 hours a day, seven days a week (24/7) and that you have the necessary bandwidth for many customers to access the site. If you self-host, your company is responsible for the cost of maintaining the server, ensuring the security of the data, and, of course, upgrading the equipment and software when necessary. Managing updates to keep your server secure and free from viruses (those nasty files you catch from the Internet that can destroy your hard drive) is an ongoing job. Very few merchants of any size host their own sites because the cost, in terms of both time and money, of managing servers, software, and telecommunications infrastructure and support is far too great.

In 1997, Angie McIntosh, a former software developer, decided to follow her passion and established Crystal Exchange America, in Middletown, Ohio, a broker of Swarovski crystal on the secondary market. Even though McIntosh knew how to host a Web site, she decided to outsource the hosting. "It just didn't make any sense for me to worry about keeping up the server on a 24-hour basis. I know what it takes, and I'd rather concentrate on the business."

Even the largest companies see the wisdom of outsourcing their hosting needs to competent, expert providers who specialize in maintaining and upgrading the infrastructure needed to ensure a safe, secure, and functional Web site. This situation is comparable to someone deciding to live in a planned community or apartment rather than own a home. Someone else carries the burden of owning the water pipes and fixing the leaks, while the occupant enjoys the advantages of living in a house.

Co-locating your server. Co-locating a server means that your company owns or leases a server, but it is physically located at a provider's facility. The co-location company handles telecommunications and day-to-day maintenance issues. However, you have responsibility for maintaining software applications and for upgrading equipment. You still need to have someone knowledgeable, either a dedicated employee or a good development and maintenance firm, to keep your site up-to-date.

Outsourced Web hosting. The vast majority of merchants with Web sites use dedicated Web-hosting firms or take advantage of the benefits of a service provider. With an outsourced solution, files that "are" the Web site sit on the provider's server and are accessed via the Internet from your com-

Outsource?

TIP Many companies feel they must host internally to protect company and client information. This is old thinking. Unless you have the in-house resources, your data is probably less secure with this internal setup. It's often more secure to co-host your server, or to outsource your hosting to a well-established firm with sound security practices. If you do decide to house the server internally, you should not store private company or client information on the server that is hooked to the Internet. This type of data should remain on a secure server, with special software, behind a firewall.

pany or by your developer whenever changes are made. What makes this option more attractive is that many service providers offer services in addition to just hosting the site, and most also provide some degree of e-commerce support. If you are a small or midsize business or are new to e-commerce, this is the best way to start. You will find the most help for the least amount of money and effort by outsourcing your hosting needs, and outsourcing will also allow you to grow in incremental steps.

There are a wide variety of Web-hosting features and e-commerce–functionality options. By selecting the elements you want, you can chose the provider that best suits your needs.

Service providers: ISPs, CSPs, ASPs, EBSPs, and other SPs. It used to be that an Internet service provider needed to do only one thing: It connected you to the Internet. But with more companies online, the explosion of e-commerce, and expanding competition, ISPs have had to expand their offerings. Internet companies are constantly reinventing, redesigning, and realigning themselves to provide more useful and focused services for their customers. In this constantly changing landscape, new companies, many with snazzy new acronyms, are working hard to differentiate themselves from the rest of the pack.

The following sections define and explain the current categories of companies and what they offer. But you should still do your homework so that you can select the company with the package of services that best fulfills your needs. Don't let the maze of options intimidate you. You can always start out small and increase the services and functionality later.

Internet service provider (ISP). An ISP in its simplest form links your computer to the Internet via a dial-up connection. Most also support your connection with minimal space for a Web site and an e-mail account or address. When you log on to the Internet from home or work through your modem and a dial-up account, you are going through an ISP.

Outsource?

Commerce service provider (CSP). A CSP is probably the easiest way for companies to operate an e-commerce–enabled Web site. A CSP is typically an ISP or Web-hosting firm that offers complete e-commerce solutions or various components that help you to build a functional e-commerce site. CSPs purchase applications from other software companies and license them out to a large member base, along with technical support. They typically offer popular Web-store software packages, such as INTERSHOP, ShopSite by Open Market, Miva Merchant, and SoftCart by Mercantec. These packages often include payment-processing services, such as CyberCash, Authorize.Net, and Payflow by VeriSign. The CSP also may offer merchant processing services, such as Cardservice International, First Data Merchant Services, Wells Fargo, Bank of America, and Bank One. These services may be necessary to complete your e-commerce site, so if they are not part of the package, you may need to purchase one separately. Examples of popular CSPs include Verio, EarthLink, and America Online (AOL).

Application service provider (ASP). Another option is to contract with an ASP. ASPs provide complete, managed, turnkey e-commerce solutions. They take on the responsibility for process, software applications, and infrastructure, but they do not necessarily provide a connection to the Internet.

There are prepackaged Web-based solutions that include everything you need to set up shop. Some are free and some you pay for. Examples of for-pay ASPs are Yahoo! Store and Amazon.com's zShops. This can be the quickest and, in the short-term, the cheapest way to get a store online. For example, Yahoo! Store costs $100 per month for up to 50 items, $300 per month for up to 1,000 items, and $100 per month for each additional 1,000 items. Using an ASP, however, gives you less flexibility in the design and functionality of your store, because you'll be limited to the framework and templates it provides.

TIP An important difference between for-pay and free ASP services is their ability to generate traffic. Fee-based Amazon-.com and Yahoo! stores are currently able to drive much more traffic to your site.

Another approach is to choose one of the new crop of free store-hosting services, such as FreeCommerce Builder by eCongo, FreeMerchant.com by Network Commerce, and Bigstep.com. These offer the basic storefront free, but charge fees for additional services.

Electronic-business service provider. E-business service providers are a new breed targeted at helping small companies jump-start their e-commerce sites. Right now, it's a little hard to differentiate them from CSPs, but EBSPs do offer additional business solutions that are needed by many small and mid-size businesses, such as payroll services, human-resource services, and legal help. The long-term goal of these newly emerging EBSPs is to help small companies integrate the Internet into their overall business processes. An EBSP walks a small business through all phases of starting and managing an e-business, including marketing and back-end systems and processes. Examples of this new generation of EBSPs are eCompany, MerchandiZer from Hip Hip Software, and Wired-2-Shop from ET Technologies. The chart on the next page will help you to understand the basic pricing differences in service providers, excluding the design and development of your site.

Design and production. Design and production of your Web site and integrated Web store can be expensive and time-consuming. The look and feel of your Web store is a critical element. As with the technical aspects of building your site, you have lots of options to choose from.

It's getting easier by the day to put together the basics of your site yourself. You no longer need to be an expert in hypertext markup language

PRICING MATRIX FOR SERVICE PROVIDERS (Monthly Fees)		
	Browser-based ASPs	**Browser-based CSPs & EBSPs**	**Custom software hosted by an ISP**
Payment services	$50 to $100	$50 to $100	$100 to $500
Web-store hosting	Free to $200	$50 to $150	$500 to $5,000
Web-site hosting	Free to $50	Free to $50	$100 to $5,000

Source: Robert Cormia/eCongo

(HTML). This programming language tells a browser how to structure a page by using a series of tags such as <Bold> and <Center> to label each instruction. If you are familiar with products such as Microsoft Office, you will easily adapt to using a WYSIWYG (what-you-see-is-what-you-get, pronounced "wizywig") creation and managing tool. Many of these packages enable you to build a Web page by using templates and by easy cutting and pasting. Designing your own site can be empowering. It can also be very time-consuming.

If you do decide to design the site yourself, creation and management tools make it quite easy and should integrate seamlessly with your current office and graphics applications. New features in the latest releases include dynamic HTML, XML (extensible mark-up language) files, and JavaScript, programs that are needed to add advanced features such as drop-down menus and rollovers. The three best-known Web-building tools are Microsoft FrontPage, Macromedia Dreamweaver 3, and Adobe PageMill®.

Macromedia and Microsoft allow you to download a 30-day free trial of their software so that you can take them for a test drive. It's a great way to get acquainted with the programs and make sure you want to take on the design task. Even if you decide not to build your own site, you will have a better idea of what is involved and how much time it should take. That information should be useful when you select a developer or designer.

If you find the off-the-shelf tools don't quite do what you had in mind, or if you don't want to spend the time designing a site, you can hire a developer. Look for someone experienced in site design and navigation, who can help with an e-commerce business and marketing plan, and who provides ongoing site maintenance and promotion. There are loads of developers out there. You want to hire one who has a background in e-commerce applications, not just a graphic designer turned Web designer. This is particularly important if you need to incorporate other business systems or dynamic catalogs. Don't forget to ask for references. Keep in mind there are organizational and cultural differences between developing an Internet-based business and the other channels with which you're probably more familiar.

Vendors that help you to create your Web site will probably be different from other resources you use. The medium, as well as the associated jargon, may take some getting used to. However, the Web industry is maturing and, with a bit of investigation, you can find a developer that fits your style.

Ash Vasudevan of Cupertino, Calif., experimented with site-building tools and felt comfortable enough to put up a Web page. But when he pictured

TIP While most hosting companies support sites developed with the tools mentioned on pages 39–40, you want to make certain your hosting company can handle files created in the tool you choose.

eCulture.com—an ethnic emporium, providing products and services such as news, culture, travel, and shopping—he realized the site would not only benefit from a professionally designed look and feel, it would also demand more than his limited knowledge to incorporate all the features he wanted. Vasudevan outsourced the development to a reputable Web designer/Webmaster, who was able to create the site he desired. The site was developed by one group and hosted by a different service provider that could help him manage growth. Once the site was built, Vasudevan took control of the daily maintenance and additions of new products and information. "I knew enough from playing with the WYSIWYG tools to be able to change information within the templates our design firm developed," Vasudevan says. "Managing the site and its content is an ongoing job, but doing it ourselves saves us a lot of money and keeps the control in-house."

The easiest design option is to use templates provided by an e-commerce service provider. These templates enable a company to design its own Web storefront by using "wizard-like" tools. Because you are limited to using

TIP You'll save yourself a lot of time and money, whether you create the site yourself or hire a developer to do it, by first reviewing other e-commerce sites. Look closely at what you consider to be functionally well-designed sites, and follow their lead. Check out their designers. There's no reason not to benefit from the experience of others. The downloadable evaluation form on the Web site of *Inc.* magazine will help you identify what works and what doesn't. (Go to www.inc.com/freetools/1,7182,CH9,00.html. Search the "Free Tool" listing for "Web Site Evaluation Worksheet.")

Outsource?

the service provider's preformatted templates, you have the least flexibility with this option. On the other hand, many of these templates are excellent, and some come with industry-specific information and readily available graphics. You can look at sample stores and take a demo tour of some of the free e-commerce service providers, such as eCongo.com, Bigstep.com, and Network Commerce. Simply log on to one of their sites and start building. It's easy. If you are prepared and have your product pictures and logos already in digital format, you should be able to build a basic store in an hour.

The cost of designing an e-commerce Web site can range from almost free (not counting your time and effort) up to hundreds of thousands of dollars. Although using a Web-design firm is more expensive than using a template, the ability to develop a Web site with exactly the look and functionality you want may be worth the extra money.

Payment processing. More than 95% of all online commerce purchases are made using a credit card, so you want to include this option in your

TIP You've probably heard of unscrupulous Web developers who overcharge their clients. There is even one story about an ISP that held a Web site hostage when its owner wanted to change services. Remember, you own your files! But there are lessons to be learned. Make sure your domain name is registered to you, not your developer. Keep yourself listed as an administrative contact with your service provider. Always ask for the original artwork back from your designer, and always keep a copy on your computer of all the files that make up your Web site. Most important, make sure you retain ownership rights to all the elements of your Web store in any contracts you sign.

design. Payment processing can be the trickiest part of putting together an e-commerce site, because it requires connecting many functions. Most of the new e-commerce service providers—ASPs, CSPs, and EBSPs—offer complete, turnkey solutions for credit-card transactions. These solutions free you from having to integrate several vendors. But you do need to shop carefully and assess the fee structures, which can vary.

Whatever you choose, just get started! As with many business decisions, time is not your friend. Would Amazon.com be the success it is if it had waited until the launch of barnesandnoble.com? Use the information in this chapter to make an initial decision whether to outsource all or part of your e-commerce Web site. Review your reasons for putting up a Web site, what your goals are, and what resources you have. Then develop a plan.

Growing into e-commerce. Don't be afraid to start with just a few Web pages. Once you have a functioning site and have staked out your e-commerce territory, you can work with your new team to decide how to best use your site to help grow your business.

Andiron Technologies, for example, offers transactionality on its site (customers are able to purchase online), but the company is facing a business problem. Although Andiron's environmentally friendly fireplace product comes in four versions, potential customers are constantly asking for customization. They e-mail questions such as "Does it come in black?," or "Can I get a double-wide version?" These requests can be fulfilled, but for a small company such as Andiron, custom orders can make the product too expensive. So Andiron's Web team has decided that the next transformation of Andiron's site will be the addition of a group-purchasing section. Online customers will be able to sign up for certain custom versions of the product. If there is enough demand for a model at the end of a specified period, the model will be produced at a price specified on the site. If the demand exceeds the level for minimum production, Andiron will be able to offer a reduced price for everyone.

Since this group-purchasing feature is not readily available through a service provider, Andiron will have to create the feature in-house. As companies engaged in e-commerce put more of their operations online, however, more service providers may offer group-purchasing features. ■

Outsource?

COMPANIES AND SITES IN THIS CHAPTER

Adobe Systems **www.adobe.com**

Amazon.com zShops **www.amazon.com**

America Online **www.aol.com**

Andiron Technologies **www.ecofire.com**

Authorize.Net **www.authorizenet.com**

Bank of America **www.bankofamerica.com**

Bank One **www.bankone.com**

barnesandnoble.com
www.barnesandnoble.com

Bigstep.com **www.bigstep.com**

Cardservice International
www.cardservice.com

CNET Networks **www.builder.com**

Crystal Exchange America
www.crystalexchange.com

CyberCash **www.cybercash.com**

EarthLink **www.earthlink.com**

ECnow.com **www.ecnow.com**

eCompany **www.ecompany.net**

eCongo.com **www.econgo.com**

eCulture.com **www.eculture.com**

ET Technologies **www.wired-2-shop.com**

First Data Merchant Services **www.firstdata.com**

HipHip Software **www.merchandizer.com**

Inc. magazine **www.inc.com**

INTERSHOP Communications **www.intershop.com**

Macromedia **www.macromedia.com**

Mercantec **www.mercantec.com**

Microsoft **www.microsoft.com**

Miva Corporation **www.miva.com**

Network Commerce **www.freemerchant.com**

Open Market **www.openmarket.com**

TopHost **www.tophost.com**

Verio **www.verio.com**

VeriSign **www.verisign.com/payment**

Wells Fargo **www.wellsfargo.com**

Yahoo! **www.store.yahoo.com**

Chapter 5

Up-front Components

The front end of your Web site is the part your customers see and interact with. It should seem familiar and understandable even if your customer isn't technically savvy. We've all been customers offline, and we know what it takes to make the buying experience smooth and successful. As in a physical store, an online store's layout should be flexible enough to suit the person who is looking for a particular item and the person who's just browsing.

The front end must greet your customers and entice them to enter your store. From the home page, your customers should be able to move around easily and intuitively. Throughout, the site should prominently show your products and services just as an in-store display would. And of course, at the end you have to make the buying process simple and efficient so that you can close the deal. All these front-end elements must work together seamlessly and effortlessly.

iPrint.com is a well-conceived site. The company communicates with its customers clearly and gives them well-priced items and efficient, high-quality service. Based in Redwood City, Calif., iPrint.com was created in 1996 by Royal P. Farros to provide easy electronic creation and ordering of popular commercially printed items such as business cards and invitations.

iPrint.com enables its customers to create professional stationery and specialty items with just a few clicks. From the time you set up your free account at iPrint.com until the products arrive at your door, iPrint.com works hard to make the shopping experience clear and simple for its customers. The iPrint.com Web site has easy-to-follow instructions that walk the user through the entire process of creating and ordering products online. Once an account is opened, iPrint.com sends an e-mail that outlines the basics of using the account, such as how to recall a design, check your order status, or reorder a product.

After you place an order, you receive a confirmation e-mail, which describes the order, confirms pricing, and gives you a reference ID so that you can check on the status of your order at any time. This e-mail also lets you know that, although the company has received authorization on your credit card, the card will not actually get charged until the order is ready to ship. When the order ships, you receive another e-mail that confirms the amount of the charge, how it was shipped, and gives you an estimated time of delivery with a hyperlink to the URL, allowing you to track the package. iPrint.com has taken a traditional industry and moved it to the Internet in a way that provides a superior customer experience.

Site building. Whether you decide to work with a developer or design the site yourself, it is imperative that you start with a map or flow chart. Just as a contractor wouldn't start work on the foundation of a house without knowing the layout, you need to build a diagram or blueprint of your site to see how the pieces fit together. Create a flow chart that follows the shopper's experience from arrival at your site through the end of the purchase. It's important to approach the storyboard from the shopper's point of view, not just through the eyes of the merchant. This flow chart will help you to organize and understand what you need to start and what you may want as you move forward.

The basic elements that the customer will see in a Web store are:
- *Home page* welcoming the customer to your Web store
- *Navigation bar* allowing the customer to move easily around the Web site
- *List of products or services* the store offers—for example, the catalog
- *Search engine* to enable the customer to locate a product or service easily and directly
- *Order form or shopping cart*
- *Tracking page* allowing the customer to determine the status of the purchase

- *Frequently asked questions (FAQs)* page to provide basic answers to questions that come up repeatedly
- *Contact page* that provides several options for contacting the company and asking for assistance

Each of these components must be designed for shopping convenience. They should incorporate attractive graphic elements that download quickly on dial-up modems as slow as 28.8K. Most important, they must be intuitively easy to use.

Home page. The home page is the first thing your customer sees when signing on to your Web site. You want to make this page engaging and informative. It's important to think about the image you want to present to your customers. Although you want to offer enough to attract their attention, the last thing you want to do is overwhelm visitors with too much at the beginning. So it's best to avoid too many graphics that can crowd the page and slow it down and to avoid a menu with too many choices.

Navigation bar. The navigation bar should allow your customer to easily access the main sections of the Web store. It is usually placed either down the left-hand side or across the top of the page. Depending on the complexity of the products or services, the "nav" bar can simply show the pages in the bullet list above, or it can have drop-down menus that display the product categories.

Catalogs and products. The manner in which you present your products or services sets the tone for the way your customers interact with your Web store. Keep in mind that almost no product is so unique it can't be found elsewhere. As with traditional selling, it's important to engage customers from the outset. They need to want to buy the product enough to go through the process of ordering online. An attractive, well-organized, and easy-to-navigate catalog is the first step to a successful Web site. A good example is the inviting entry into the Crate & Barrel Web store on the next page.

Because the Web is nonlinear and your customers can move from page to page in a number of ways, the design of your online catalog should be approached differently from the way you would approach a paper catalog. The ability to move around traditional "departments" must be rethought in the context of an online store. The same merchandise can be sorted in a number of ways simultaneously. Say you stock a women's navy jacket that packs well. In your store you'd have to decide whether to put it in women's wear, sportswear, or vacationwear. But on the Web it can be in all three places at once, and also listed under "navy" to be easily matched with an outfit. If a red shirt or a red sweater would be equally acceptable for the consumer, the ability to search for a red "top" must be available. Remember to keep thinking like your customers.

Product information. It's a good idea to make as much information about your products as possible available to your shoppers. This includes physical characteristics, (sizes, colors, measurements, power requirements), as well as product availability, ship dates, special fees, and so forth. The more easily and accurately the Web site provides answers to a shopper's questions, the more likely it is the shopper will close the deal.

Try to think of your Web site as a personal shopper for each buyer. What would it be like if everyone entering your store had a dedicated salesperson? Imagine which questions and issues would arise. Having the answers to the questions easily available to the shopper will ensure a more successful shopping experience. However, it is also important to keep in mind that the information should not overwhelm the shopper. Think of it this way: If a shopper in your store asks what horsepower a small engine produces, he or she doesn't want hear about the number of parts in the engine, where it was made, its recommended uses, and product warnings before getting the answer. The customer wants to know what the horsepower is. Of course, the next customer may well have a different set of questions. A good salesperson knows all about your inventory, but will tell the customer only what is appropriate for that particular transaction. Create your Web site to use the same philosophy. Thorough information should be easily available, but not presented all at once.

Product images. A picture is worth a thousand words, and having clear pictures of your products can make the difference between securing and losing a sale. Whenever an image is used on a Web site, the designer must take into consideration its file size and, therefore, the length of time to download the image. One sure way to lose a shopper's attention is to make him or her wait too long to see the product. The size and resolution of each image must

be considered carefully so that it is clear enough for the shopper to evaluate the product, but small enough to download quickly. One approach is initially to present the shopper with "thumb-nail" photos, which can be clicked on to be enlarged, such as those above on the garden.com site.

Catalog maintenance. One of the advantages of a Web-based catalog is that changes are relatively easy to make. Once a paper catalog is printed, it's impossible to change anything in that edition. With a Web-based catalog, any element can be adjusted as needed. However, this does mean that site maintenance can be an ongoing task. There are two sides to Web-site maintenance—the nontechnical content management and the technical task of transforming the product images and information into HTML so that your customers can receive them on the Internet.

Depending on how frequently you update your online catalog or product listings, the technical task can be a full-time job. If you think it's likely you will need this level of support, be sure to include the cost in the Web-store budget.

While most Web-based site-building tools require manual entry of each item, some have the capability of receiving an entire catalog from Excel, Access, and other spreadsheet and database programs. You'll want this feature if your business has multiple items or SKUs.

If you outsource the technical elements of your Web store, it is crucial that you have a clear understanding of the level of maintenance available to you from the vendor. If you will need changes made to the site weekly, make sure your vendor can handle a fast turnaround. If you have a lot of text or pictures to scan, discuss how long it takes to convert them to HTML. A clear understanding of how much and how often you'll update the site is of utmost importance when you plan your resources.

Another thing to think about when planning your site maintenance is the nature of your catalog. Catalogs can be static or dynamic. The majority of catalogs on the Web are static pages that are changed manually on an individual basis. A dynamic catalog is connected directly to your product database and is automatically updated whenever there is a change in the file. This system is better for notifying customers when items are available and for removing products from the site when they are out of stock. However, managing a dynamic Web catalog is not for the beginner. You will need to enlist the help of a professional developer. But if you handle numerous products and fluctuating inventory levels, a dynamic catalog may be your best answer and worth the extra investment.

Selling and delivering digital content. Selling over the Internet is not limited to physical products that you ship to your customer. It also includes digital products. A prime example comes from the software industry, which has led the way with the digital download of software programs. Electronic software distribution (ESD) has served as a basis for the sale and transfer of other digital goods, such as music, art, books, and tickets for airlines or events.

Primary considerations for electronically distributed sales are bandwidth, security, and, of course, tracking (see Chapter 8). Customers and end users need a means of fast access, such as digital subscriber line (DSL), cable modem, T-1, or ISDN line, to adequately take advantage of digital distribution. As the technology catches up and people have higher bandwidth capabilities, the selling of digital content over the Internet will grow.

Depending on your product or service, you may want to consider a digital component after a while. For instance, if your company makes gourmet doggie biscuits, the basis of your business is in physically delivering the biscuits. But if you decide to expand to add dog-training videos to your product mix, digital delivery may be a viable and inexpensive option for you. It will certainly save you money on packaging, handling, and shipping costs.

Search engines and shopping carts. A search engine is software that searches through data on the Web, looking for specific words or phrases. You should consider adding a search engine so visitors can search the content of your Web site. Search engines allow customers to go directly to the product they want, without going through layers of categories. Depending on the complexity of your Web store, the search engine included with most store-building software will probably suit your needs. More-sophisticated search engines can offer suggestions for alternative or complementary products, in addition to the item that was initially searched for.

On the Web, the shopping cart is software that allows the shopper to select and save a series of items for purchase. Shopping-cart software is available for purchase or license if you are building your own site, or integrated as part of the e-commerce package if you choose to outsource the e-commerce elements of your Web site.

Statistics show that more than two-thirds of online customers abandon shopping carts before completing their purchases. It's not always because of a last-minute change of heart. Studies show that difficult ordering and payment processes are the biggest deterrents to online shopping. All shopping carts are not alike. Some offer advanced features and display more information, resulting in a smoother shopping experience. With some carts, for example, the shopper can see what is in the cart only by clicking on it, while other software allows the shopper to view the contents at all times. Some shopping carts make it difficult to make more than one purchase at a time. Displaying shipping charges and applicable taxes are helpful features not available in some packages. It is important to anticipate your shoppers' needs and to select a shopping cart that best fits them. If a customer can't figure out how to make a purchase from you, he or she will make it from someone else.

drugstore.com, a site that offers thousands of health and beauty products, has a particularly well-conceived shopping cart. When the first item is selected, an explanation of the shopping cart is displayed, clarifying all the features of the cart and how additional items will be treated. This display appears the first time you order. When you return to the site, cookies cause the site to recognize and welcome you by name, and the shopping-cart information isn't displayed again unless you click for more details. This shopping cart is always on view at the left side of the page so that shoppers can keep track of what they have ordered.

One of the extra customer-experience elements at the drugstore.com site is a list feature. Recognizing that many products purchased in drugstores are bought regularly, each item you buy from the site is placed on a list that is available to you every time you visit so that you can reorder without having to go through the regular steps of searching or browsing. The list even has an e-mail reminder option the shopper can set to send purchase messages at selected time intervals, every two weeks, six months, and so on. Tied in with shopping-cart software, these features make shopping much more convenient and personalized.

Cart features. Basic features of a good, integrated shopping cart include:

- Product name and SKU (stock-keeping unit)
- Pricing and quantity fields
- The ability to add or delete items
- Calculation of taxes, shipping, and handling
- Ability to purchase several items in the same session by leaving the shopping cart and continuing to shop
- Secure purchasing
- Order confirmation
- Reporting

Optional advanced features might include:

- Ability to handle foreign currency
- Multiple-region tax calculation
- Multiple reporting

Customer-service tools. Your Web site should eventually incorporate features that increase the customer's control over the purchase experience. The more current the information you make available and the easier you make the exchange of information, the more likely you are to have a return customer.

One feature of a fully operational e-commerce site is the ability to incorporate other business elements into the Web site. If your front end and back end are integrated, you can tell your customers about the availability of any product in real time. You can also let them know when a product is on order, the expected arrival (and therefore shipping) date, and if something has been discontinued. As with any sales transaction, clear, fast, honest communication is appreciated by the customer and will bring that customer back again.

It is important to enable your customers to check the status of their orders directly from the Internet. Your site should generate a tracking number whenever a purchase is made so that the order can be followed by any services involved in the shipment. Gateway, the direct-seller of computers, assigns each order a number. Buyers have the option of going to the Gateway site and entering their order or phone number to see the estimated shipping date for each item in their order.

Frequently asked questions (FAQs). Another common Web feature that saves time and effort is a frequently asked questions (FAQ) page, which can provide answers to questions customers ask repeatedly. The page should be equipped with a search capability so that the shopper can find the exact piece of information required. Making standard information, such as return policies, security measures, and company history, accessible on the Web site can also save a lot of customer-service time and money.

Contact page. You should always clearly post at least one means by which customers can contact you. More than one is preferable. The customer's ability to get in touch with the merchant is often what saves a sale that's run into problems. E-mail is the most common method of communication. A "mail to" button that pops up a blank message form addressed to someone in your company can be put on any page. You can also post a toll-free contact phone number or a mailing address.

It is critical that you respond quickly to inquiries sent to you from your customers. Don't let e-mails pile up in your inbox any more than you would ignore phone messages. There are e-mail programs that include automated-response systems and customer-relationship management, which can be a good option. These are discussed further in the next chapter.

Credit cards. The vast majority of purchases on the Internet are made with credit cards. For purposes of this book, let's assume you are generally familiar with offline credit-card processing. In Chapter 6, you will find a diagram that reviews the credit-card transaction as it passes from the customer, over the Internet, into your merchant account.

Fraud. An Internet credit-card transaction is identical to a credit card transaction over the counter, with one big exception. The merchant can't ask for personal identification. Most publicity that surrounds credit-card fraud over the Internet revolves around a consumer's privacy rights and the probability that the individual's credit-card number will be stolen. In fact, the risk is far greater to the merchant than to the consumer. In most cases, the consumer has a $50 limit to liability provided by the card issuer. The merchant, however, is ultimately responsible if the merchandise is shipped and the transaction turns out to be fraudulent.

There are safeguards that most e-commerce site providers use to lessen the chances of fraudulent transactions. One benefit of outsourcing your store to a service provider is that the host simultaneously gathers data from numerous stores and therefore has a far larger pool of information against which to check any individual transaction. If a card number shows signs of misuse, their systems are triggered to "scrub" by cross-checking the card's validity, including checking with the issuing company.

Customer tracking. It is imperative that you quickly confirm any order placed by a customer. There is nothing worse for a buyer than to feel an order has gone into the Internet ether. It is also smart to capture customer information for marketing purposes. However, it is good business practice to give the customer an opportunity to "opt out" of receiving marketing materials.

Capturing customer data on a well-designed Web site allows you to send customers personalized and appropriate information. You can gather facts essential for properly identifying a customer in various ways. One way is to require your customers to fill out a registration form in order to shop at your site. However, if someone thinks you are asking too much, that person may just click away to another site. In order to balance the scales, consider offering an incentive for filling out the form, such as an

TIP A cookie is a little file sent to the viewer's computer by your Web server (host). It contains information that can be retrieved by the server at a later time, when it enables the server to recognize the shopper. Cookies are used to identify and track shoppers and can be a benefit to the user as well. Cookies can keep track of passwords and preferences and can automatically customize the appearance of your Web site.

Some customers, however, do not want cookies on their computers. Both Internet Explorer and Netscape browsers allow the creation of cookies, but the user can specify that a prompt appear before a cookie is placed on the hard drive. That way, the user can accept or reject the cookie.

online coupon or access to a special part of the site.

Another way to gather customer information is to use a cookie. A cookie is a small file that sits on the user's computer and allows your Web site to recognize the user. Although this level of communication with your customer is optimal, it is an element that might be more appropriately introduced at a later stage in your Web store's development.

E-commerce product-comparison matrix. Many competent vendors and service providers offer the latest e-commerce tools, so comparison shopping can be overwhelming, especially when you're just beginning. Filling out a matrix can help you analyze the available functions and features. To download an e-commerce product-comparison matrix, go to www.inc.com/freetools/1,7182,CHL9,00.html. Then search the "Free Tool" listing for "E-commerce Product Matrix." The matrix will help you decide what features you need on your e-commerce Web site and will allow you to compare the features offered by several service providers. Filling out the matrix is a good first step in planning the up-front components of your site. The other half of an e-commerce Web site (the back-office components) is covered in the next chapter. ■

COMPANIES AND SITES
IN THIS CHAPTER

Crate & Barrel **www.crateandbarrel.com**
drugstore.com **www.drugstore.com**
garden.com **www.garden.com**
Gateway **www.gateway.com**
iPrint.com **www.iPrint.com**

Chapter 6

Back-office Components

Building the Web store is, of course, just the beginning. Until the customer gets what he or she paid for and you get the money, the transaction is not complete. This all happens at the "back end."

There are two ways to approach the back end of the transaction. The Web store can be set up so that all back-end operations are separate from the forms and processes used by the customer. In this case, your Web store notifies you only that an order has been placed. You then bring into play whatever processes already exist in your business to get the products to the customer. As discussed in Chapter 3, this is how many small and midsize businesses make their initial forays into e-commerce. However, most Web-store packages offered by ASPs and CSPs include tools that integrate the front end of your Web store directly into your back-office business processes. Using them to full advantage saves considerable time and money.

Areas of your business that can be integrated with the site include:

- *Payment processing*
- *Taxes*
- *Shipping and tracking*
- *Inventory management*
- *Fulfillment and logistics*
- *Sales-reporting tools*
- *Customer-support management*

Payment processing. Payments are the heart of online commerce. For many merchants, handling this process is a quick introduction to the complexities of conducting transactions in a "credit-card-not-present" environment. As mentioned in Chapter 4, almost all online purchases are made using a credit card, so it is important to set up an accurate and responsive system. Fortunately, credit-card processing for Internet merchants has become an easy-to-integrate turnkey process.

ONLINE CREDIT-CARD TRANSACTION

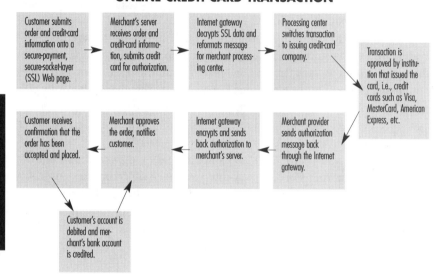

Back Office

Start with the bank that already handles your business and is therefore familiar with you and your credit needs. If you don't want to work with your current bank, larger institutions, such as Wells Fargo, Bank of America, Citibank, and Bank One, have Internet initiatives, including credit-card processing. You need a U.S. bank account (or an account in the country in which you do business) and a decent credit history. If you are a mail-order business, you might be able to apply for a merchant account you can use for both phone and Web-based transactions. More likely, you're a bricks-and-mortar business, and the terms of your account may specifically prohibit card-not-present transactions. You need to alter this arrangement in order to fully engage in e-commerce.

There are three pieces to the credit-card payment process. The first piece is the merchant acquiring institution, often known as the original service provider (OSP). Of these, the best known are Cardservice International, First Data Merchant Services, and traditional providers, including Wells Fargo and Bank of America. The second piece is the payment gateway, a mechanism that transmits the data from the customer's shopping cart to the OSP. Some key providers here are CyberCash and Authorize.Net. The third piece is your traditional merchant bank account, which must be an American bank for processing within the United States. The diagram on the previous page shows how these three pieces interact to complete a credit-card transaction.

Whether your transaction system is supplied by separate vendors or by one turnkey package, make sure you carefully read the terms of service, which will describe the costs associated with each step. There is a monthly lease fee for the merchant account itself, which may or may not include fees associated with access to the payment gateway. Purchased separately, gateway fees charged by organizations such as CyberCash are about $40 per month. Minimum processing fees may apply if you do not exceed a minimum threshold (typically, $500 per month). There are also per-transaction fees of about $0.30, which, combined with the discount rate of about 2.5% to 3.0%, add up to a minimum processing fee of about $20 per month. There may also be statement fees of $10 to $15 per month. All together, your credit-card processing cost could be as little as $15 per month or as high as $100. Check your documentation and compare it with the matrix on the next page.

CREDIT-CARD PROCESSING PRICE MATRIX

Monthly payment	Varies from $15 to $50 per month
Discount rate	Ranges from about 2.5% to 3.0%
Payment gateway access	Can be included, or up to $40 per month
Per-transaction fee	Averages $0.25 to $0.30 per transaction
Minimum processing fee	About $20 per month; varies with vendor
Monthly report fee	Can be included, or up to $10 per month

Security. Security and encryption are crucial to a Web store. Encryption is the translation of data into a secret code, which scrambles the information with a mathematical formula that is nearly impossible to decipher without the proper key or password. Encryption is implemented by using technologies such as secure sockets layer (SSL), which was developed by Netscape for transmitting private documents via the Internet. SSL and SHTML (secure-HTML) work by using a private key to encrypt data that is transferred over the secure connection. Both Netscape Navigator and Internet Explorer support SSL, and many Web sites use the protocol to ensure security when they ask for confidential user information, such as credit-card numbers. By convention, Web pages that require an SSL connection start with https instead of http.

Verification. With all Internet sales, the seller needs to make sure the buyer has a valid credit card. Payment vendors that have staked an Internet claim are experts at security and authentication for software and other digital sales. Whichever solution you choose, make sure your provider does some form of "fraud scrub." This process helps prevent stolen or illegally forged credit-card numbers from being used to purchase goods.

Other payment options. As in a physical shopping experience, there are payment options other than credit cards that can be used to complete this portion of the transaction. There are also several new electronic payment forms developed specifically for Internet payments, such as PayPal (see Chapter 3), which are being used by some auction sites. These payment options include check or money order sent via e-mail, micropayments, digital cash, electronic checks, escrow services, and debit cards.

Taxes. You've most likely heard that Internet sales are not taxed. Don't be fooled. There is a legal term, *nexus*, which roughly means that wherever you have a presence doing business, you are obligated to collect and report taxes. So you still need to pay taxes on your eligible online sales—at least in any state in which you have a physical presence. For example, if your manufacturing plant is in California and you have a representative in New Jersey, you are liable for taxes in both California and New Jersey. As a matter of course, you should check with your accountant and/or tax attorney to determine for which states you need to collect taxes.

Tax liability is quite confusing, with more than 50,000 separate tax zones in the United States. There are hundreds of sales-tax zones in California alone. To start, there is the state tax, but most counties have an additional rate, and some cities have yet another tax on top of the rest. If your customer resides in San Francisco, the tax rate is 8.5%. But if he or she lives a short drive across a bridge, he may be paying 7.25% in Marin or 8.25% in Berkeley.

If you sell different types of items, you need to allow for products that are taxable, as well as those that are tax-exempt. In California, for instance, most food is not subject to tax, but clothing is. In New Jersey, however, clothing is not taxed.

Luckily, several services and software solutions can automate your tax calculations. If you are building your e-commerce site from scratch, you can either purchase a package from a company such as TAXWARE International or take advantage of an online system such as CyberSource. If you use a solution from your e-commerce service provider, it is likely the provider has an integrated tax-calculation package. Make sure the system calculates taxes per region rather than taxes based on one standard statewide tax rate.

Shipping. If you sell products, you need to ship them. National shippers have realized they are integral to the entire Internet-commerce supply chain, so they have moved aggressively to develop Web-based tracking services to establish relationships with major regional distribution centers and to offer deliveries seven days a week. Shippers have also integrated customer-service elements into their online services and can link a configuration screen to your Web or physical store to coordinate shipping and delivery.

New Internet companies are entering this market as well, to help Web merchants with their shipping needs. For example, Stamps.com has acquired a complete interface for calculating shipping rates using any of the major ship-

TIP The logistics of calculating tax, shipping, and tracking, plus your accrued state liabilities, are no longer just programs you load on your computer. They are fully integrated in many Web-based, e-commerce service providers' offerings, or the shopper can link to them through his/her own browser.

ping providers. IShip.com, a service of Stamps.com, makes shipping simple by putting all the information for multiple carriers in one easy-to-use Web page.

As discussed previously, these tools are also excellent customer-support resources, allowing the customer to check the status of items without any effort from the merchant. Advanced versions of these tools, which are generally available for people or companies that ship more than 10 packages a day, allow you to generate management reports on shipping expenses and activity and allow you to export data to customs officials electronically.

Inventory. Inventory management for merchants with Web stores can become automated by linking an application database to your catalog. This is not a task for beginners, because it requires an understanding of the workings of a database (Access, SQL, Oracle, DB2, or Informix) running on an application server that is logically connected to the site. Many higher-end Web-hosting portals and more sophisticated packaged software from such vendors as Open Market (ShopSite) and INTERSHOP Communications, and CSPs offering the Kurant StoreSense solution can supply this ability. These packages, in addition to some of the ASP offerings, have incremental counters that change the inventory shown on the Web site as items are ordered, so quantities are calculated in real time. Take time to ask your provider whether this feature is available. Reviews in print and online of products and Web-store services can provide leads to the most complete vendors.

Linking your legacy systems (older computer-software programs) to your e-commerce applications can require a fair amount of database programming, which for larger merchants can easily cost $5,000 or more. If you are trying to link in your legacy systems, it might be wise to find a data center or professional-services organization to do custom integration. These services are usually priced at more than $125 per hour.

Fulfillment. Getting the correct product out the door to the customer in a timely fashion is the next crucial element of e-commerce. Fulfillment is often the area in which merchants win or lose the battle for customer loyalty. As we discussed in Chapter 5, the customer should be able to track each step of the fulfillment process, including merchant-order notification, communication to the warehouse, and shipping information. To round out your system, look for a solution that automatically updates the status in the customer-account file.

Automation of the shipping process is one of the benefits of Web technology. There are times, however, when you need personal attention. The case is well stated by Corinne Moore, CEO of Chocoholic.com, a Redwood City, Calif., company that sells gourmet chocolate—a highly perishable product that Moore ships around the U.S. "We soon learned that our complete ordering system needed human intervention for checks and balances. You can imagine what happens to chocolate if it sits in a steamy warehouse in Georgia or bakes on a hot afternoon in the back of a courier vehicle. It melts! Our system allows people to choose between next-day delivery, two-day delivery, and traditional ground service. But in the hot summer months or if we know we are shipping to a warm climate, we must ship by the fastest means available."

Reporting. Various reporting tools and techniques are available to the builder of a Web store and are essential for every online business. Options for tracking and reporting are discussed in Chapter 8.

Besides generating reports on your customers' viewing or online shopping habits, many hosting packages offer standard reports on sales by payment type, such as the sample on the next page.

Customer-management tools. There are two elements to successful customer management. The first is the ability to respond to your customers' questions and complaints in a timely manner. The second is managing the information about your customers and understanding their preferences. Just

SAMPLE ONLINE SALES REPORT

Month Ending	10/31/1999	11/30/1999	12/31/1999	1/31/2000	2/29/2000	3/31/2000	4/30/2000
Page Views	2,945	19,466	16,780	15,226	13,140	37,070	39,512
Customers	1,480	9,577	9,011	8,474	6,537	22,755	19,840
Page Views/Customer	1.99	2.03	1.86	1.8	2.01	1.63	1.99
Orders	42	115	82	114	78	122	144
Income	2,236.05	3,736.10	4,025.40	6,044.94	3,691.54	5,843.66	7,237.22
Items Sold	66	203	170	255	136	219	227
Average order	53.24	32.49	49.09	53.03	47.33	47.90	50.26

Source: Yahoo! Store

as in the bricks-and-mortar world, you will lose customers if you don't respond to them in an informative and timely way. But because the Internet is such an instant communication medium, your customers expect even faster service—in most cases, same-day answers.

Feeling overwhelmed? Relax. Technology can help with automatic e-mail response systems and with systems to manage and store your customer information. Services such as eGain Mail automatically sort, prioritize, and respond to basic e-mail queries. Protect yourself by forwarding each e-mail to two addresses. This will make certain that if one server crashes, you can still recover your correspondence. Think about which departments need to see the message. Use database software to track responses to ensure that every e-mail is answered and that you don't answer the same e-mail message twice. Programs such as iKnowWeb can help you to create online searchable FAQs, which supply answers to common queries. More advanced e-mail programs come with an auto response that assigns a tracking number so that you can access the case if there is a problem or if the customer decides to pick up the phone.

Tools like these and the new customer-relationship management (CRM) tools help companies integrate their customer information throughout the organization by linking customer information and inventory databases. Properly shared and analyzed among various departments, such as marketing, sales, and service, this constantly updated data allows all departments to work with the latest information. Companies must know who their customers are, which customer populations are driving their profits, and what will keep these customers happy and loyal. ■

Back Office

COMPANIES AND SITES IN THIS CHAPTER

Authorize.Net **www.authorize.com**

Bank of America **www.bankofamerica.com**

Bank One **www.bancone.com**

Cardservice International **www.cardservice.com**

Chocoholic.com **www.chocoholic.com**

Citibank **www.citibank.com**

CyberCash **www.cybercash.com**

CyberSource **www.cybersource.com**

eGain Communications **www.egain.com**

First Data Merchant Services **www.firstdata.com**

INTERSHOP Communications **www.intershop.com**

Knowlix **www.knowlix.com**

Open Market **www.openmarket.com**

PayPal **www.paypal.com**

Stamps.com **www.stamps.com**

TAXWARE International **www.taxware.com**

Wells Fargo **www.wellsfargo.com**

Chapter 7

The Online Shopping Experience

S hopping in the virtual world is, in many ways, identical to shopping in the real world. The wants and needs that motivate customers to walk through your door are the same forces that will drive them to your Web site. The famous online book seller Amazon.com is cited as an excellent example of an e-commerce site because of its ability to appeal to different types of shoppers. From the first page, a shopper can search for a specific item, navigate to other pages that accommodate browsing by category, or look through a special gift section that combines various categories. Once shoppers get further into the site and find a particular item, customer reviews provide extra information to assist with the buy decision. There are also specific recommendations for alternative or extra items, as well as lists of top sellers, special bargains, and free downloads.

The result of all this attention to the customer is that Amazon.com does not need to compete on price. In fact, despite its popularity, it is rarely the lowest price option. Nevertheless, customers choose to return to Amazon.com because of the high level of customer service and support, plus the huge selection of items.

Customer attractions. The best e-merchants know how to maximize the elements that attract customers to purchase a product, and they work hard to control things that may deter a sale. The following factors are currently persuading an increasing number of shoppers to buy online:

• *Convenience.* The most obvious factor that brings shoppers to the Internet is the sheer ease of shopping. A potential customer can decide to shop as soon as his computer is online. Several techniques can help you capitalize on this convenience. Search engines that allow for both keyword and quick searches will appeal to more shoppers than search engines with just one function. Input systems that distinguish between "bill to" and "ship to" addresses are classy and save time. E-mail notices that remind shoppers to replenish staples or alert them to special offers can be very effective in encouraging repeat business. Extra conveniences will keep your customers and clients coming back to shop at your site.

• *Privacy.* The privacy that online shopping provides is a boon to many shoppers. Obviously, this is particularly important for non-mainstream items. There are any number of reasons why people may want to keep a purchase private. For instance, they may have some embarrassment about the product or service they are buying. One popular drugstore site has a television commercial that features an uncomfortable customer asking a young clerk for a constipation remedy. Shoppers with some medical conditions may want to keep them from their neighbors, co-workers, or local salespeople. People in these and other sensitive situations appreciate the confidentiality the Internet provides. You should assure your shoppers that their personal information is secure and will only be used internally. This is the key to giving your shoppers peace of mind and turning them into repeat customers. You can also create a deeper level of trust among your customers by belonging to organizations such as TRUSTe and BBB*OnLine*.

• *Broad product and merchant selection.* The ease with which a Web store can be set up, plus the feeling that it is an important sales channel, has merchants flocking to the Internet. E-commerce is in its infancy, and already there are more online stores than anyone can count. If you're looking for the perfect Japanese wedding kimono, odds are you'll find it somewhere on the Internet.

While this huge selection is a boon for the shopper, it does challenge you as an online merchant to make your store stand out from the crowd. On the other hand, creative marketing can drive visitors and customers to your site. (This subject is covered in Volume 1 of this series, *Tips & Tactics for*

Marketing on the Internet.) Along with marketing, you need to devote your efforts to customer retention—making sure your customers come back. Keeping your Web site up to date and stocked with new items is critical. Changing your material entices people to come back often to see what's new. If you provide a service instead of sell a product, free information and guidance for your customers can help to keep your site in their minds.

• *Competitive pricing and tax avoidance.* Many shoppers started their online shopping practices mainly because of the opportunity to save money. The proliferation of Web-only stores that can operate with reduced overhead costs has created a pool of reduced-price products on the Internet. When a shopping comparison search brings up five lawnmowers with different costs, competing on price becomes an important sales strategy. Monitoring and matching your competitors' prices, offering free or reduced shipping, and offering discounts and specials should be considered an integral part of your online pricing strategy.

Many companies started their Web presence with the establishment of a Web "outlet," which serves two positive goals. It can get rid of excess

TIP As with shopping in any store, trust is established through positive encounters. Word of mouth is the most compelling reason for people to visit a Web site. A recent report from Jupiter Communications, an Internet research and analysis firm based in New York, found that most people pass information about a site to between four and six of their friends. As more customers have positive online shopping experiences, word of mouth will bring more shoppers to your Web-based door.

inventory easily and cheaply, and it gets customers back to your site repeatedly to check out the new discounts. Of course, it is important to make sure you don't undercut the image of your Web site. Not everyone can or should compete on price alone. If the image you want to project is of upscale luxury and elegance, other elements, such as exclusivity, are likely to be your edge.

• *Market and product research.* One of the strongest motivators for shoppers is the sheer wealth of product information available online. Many Web sites, such as CNET, ZDNet, and Consumer Reports Online, include product reviews. Recently opened Web sites, such as Epinions, let consumers post their own reviews of the products and services they have purchased. Also, many stores provide supporting information about their products. For consumers who like to research and comparison shop before making a purchase, the Internet is a dream.

• *Fun and enjoyment.* Online shopping is fun! The novelty alone is enough to get some customers to try it. And receiving a delivery is like getting a present, even if you did buy it yourself. Shopping, in general, is an activity many of us do for enjoyment, regardless of where and in what fashion. The Internet expands the opportunities.

Many Web sites have incorporated entertainment elements into their Web sites to capitalize on the fun factor. Companies have added contests, quizzes, and online chats. Some sites are extremely successful in creating repeat business with these elements. Keep in mind, however, that not all shoppers are interested in the extras and might stay away from sites that offer too many diversions. On the other hand, do not ignore the possibility of a new revenue stream that can be developed from advertisements on the nonessential areas of your Web site.

Customer deterrents. Just as technology has increased the speed of the Internet, it has reduced the time it takes to turn a customer on or off. Studies indicate that as many as 66% of online shopping expeditions are dropped mid-stride. And while many of these shoppers will return to the Internet, it is unlikely they will return to a Web store that has turned in a poor performance. Several things can lead to a disappointing shopping experience:

- *Slow Web performance.* You run the risk of losing a customer at the very beginning if your Web page loads too slowly. Customers won't even bother to stick around to see the beautifully designed home page you worked so hard to create. Even if you have optimized the page so that it loads quickly, success can bite you. If you get too many people to visit your site and you don't have enough bandwidth on your servers to handle the crowd, the page loads slowly and shoppers leave quickly. The potential for this problem increases if it's a heavy day on the shoppers' ISP or with your service provider. Regardless of the cause, a slow site is deadly. It is crucial that you closely track the performance of your Web site. A number of services provide performance information, including Keynote Systems.

- *Product availability.* No one likes to be teased, but online stores do it all the time. It is important that you do not offer products or services that are currently not available to the shopper. Dynamically connecting your inventory to your Web store is one way to solve this problem.

- *Lack of sensory experience.* Many people don't like shopping online because they can't touch and hold the products. Some merchandise will always be sold more successfully in person. As people get used to buying over the Internet and buying habits change to prioritize convenience over the tactile experience, this will not be as great a factor as it is today. Incentives can tip the scales toward a shopper's actually making a purchase online. Making customers aware of your liberal return policy by posting it prominently on your site can help alleviate some customer hesitancy about purchasing certain products.

- *Lack of "mall experience and entertainment."* Shopping is frequently a social experience. When you go shopping, you see and interact with other people. The input you experience during a trip to mall stimulates all five senses (especially if you stop for a snack). Online shopping uses, at most, two senses, and that's only if the Web site has multimedia elements so that a shopper hears things as well as sees them.

• *Lack of adequate customer service.* One of the most common complaints about real-life stores is that there are never enough salespeople. Well, there are virtually none on the Internet. (Voice-over Internet technology, which allows shoppers to speak to a live customer-support person, is showing up on some larger sites, but at the moment very few online businesses use it.) Currently, the customer must instigate almost all customer-service activities—and it is usually with a written message, not in a conversation. And all too often, the response is slow in coming, if it comes at all. Jupiter Communications reports that 27% of customer-service requests went unanswered during holiday season 1999. Obviously, it is important to make sure the online shopping experience is always positive. If, for some reason, the experience is less than positive, go the extra mile to make up for real problems and also for perceived slights. Unfortunately, this is one area in which the gap between customer expectations and industry performance is wide.

TIP One way to give your Web store dimension is to give customers the opportunity to read and write product reviews on your site. Another is to create an area on your site for an online community or chat group. Of course, whether this is appropriate depends on the nature of the service or product you sell.

• *Perceived security concerns.* While credit-card transactions are safe, there is a growing concern about sending the information over the Internet. Recent thefts of credit-card information from online merchants have only increased customers' anxiety, even though the theft did not occur during the transmission of data. Although studies indicate that these fears are declining, you must still consider them. Offer your customers alternative payment methods to complete the transaction. Make sure your credit-card transactions are handled on a secure server and print that assurance right on your site. (Surprisingly, many credit-card transactions are not protected this way.) Membership in the organizations mentioned earlier, TRUSTe and BBB*OnLine*, can also help to bolster your image with regard to security.

• *Orders not filled on time.* It is easy to put a catalog on the Internet. It is much harder to make sure all the business processes behind your Web store are coordinated with the page your customer sees. One of the biggest problems with online shopping is that items are not shipped immediately. Many people shop online because of the perceived immediacy of the process. If they haven't gotten a gift with enough time to wrap and ship it, many shoppers turn to the Internet to speed things along. Remember the lesson Toys "R" Us learned during the 1999 holiday season? It sent out thousands of dollars in $100 gift certificates to customers whose merchandise didn't arrive in time for Christmas. If the company's back-end databases had been integrated with its Web site, customers would have known immediately whether the products were available.

• *Uncertainty and lack of order notification.* A major deterrent to online purchasing is an ordering system that is unclear about when a purchase was made. There are plenty of customers who press the "Submit" button twice and end up with twice the items they want. Or they are so uncertain the order was placed that they go through the entire process again. Other people back out of placing an order because they aren't sure at which point they are committed to paying for the merchandise. It is imperative

BEST PRACTICES: WHAT'S COOL ABOUT J. CREW

The J. Crew Web site provides an excellent shopping experience for its customers. The site has a clean, sophisticated look consistent with its overall image. As with many good marketing efforts, the site sells a lifestyle as much as it does clothes. The home page is uncluttered, but it still offers a lot of information. It has pictures of featured items and direct links to several key pages in the Web site, as well as other elements.

This site excels in the area of navigation. Customers can choose to move through the site using a navigation bar at the top of the page, "hot" links to the main content index in the center graphic, and a second nav bar at the bottom of the page. Once you are at the main index of items, sub-navigation elements appear. When an item is selected, the navigation bar that describes all the items in a segment—shirts/cotton stretch, for example—are still visible in case the shopper wants to display another shirt. All the colors offered are displayed in small pictures that can be enlarged.

The shopping cart is simple and easy to complete. The checkout form has its security policy stated in a large box at the top of the page. Within seconds of completing an order, a pop-up screen displays an order-tracking number that can be used from then on.

Among other especially well-designed sites are these (see the box at the end of the chapter for URLs):

Amazon.com	Game Express	Reel.com
At Home Corporation	Kozmo.com	Webvan Group
drugstore.com	Proflowers.com	

that you provide accurate and sufficient information at every stage of the process. Making sure your system provides an order-tracking number and giving it to your customer goes a long way to reassuring the customer.

Key technical factors. The following is a brief overview of elements that contribute to an excellent online shopping experience.

Initial greet page
- Fast loading
- Engaging design and information

Navigation
- Easy to understand
- Consistent on each page

Qualifying the customer
- Registration for customers who will return (but this should not be a requirement to enter your site unless you want to restrict tire-kickers)

Pre-sale assistance
- Enough information available, including contact information, to allow your customer to make a valid decision

Presenting the product
- A clear, but quickly loading, image of the product
- Easy access to a description of the product attributes

Shopping-cart functionality
- Easy to understand
- Easy to use

Order processing
- Secure credit-card processing
- Shipping details
- Tracking capabilities and connections

Customer service and support
- Initial response to customer inquiry within 24 hours
- Follow up with full response as soon as possible
- More than one way to contact you

Shortest shopping path
- Good catalog design
- Search capabilities
- Ability to order from any point

Privacy/policy statements
- Clear statement of privacy policy
- Stick to what you promise to do with customer information

As online customers' expectations reach new heights, it is important that your Web site is the best you can afford in terms of both design and functionality. There is a low tolerance for failure among Web shoppers. Address your customers' needs with multiple types of customer support, and do all you can to deliver on time and to respond promptly. In short, entice customers. Make online shopping easy; make it fast; and make it secure. ∎

COMPANIES AND SITES IN THIS CHAPTER

Amazon.com **www.amazon.com**

At Home Corporation **www.bluemountain.com**

BBBOnLine **www.bbbonline.org**

CNET **www.cnet.com**

Consumer Reports Online
www.consumerreports.org

drugstore.com **www.drugstore.com**

Epinions **www.epinions.com**

Game Express **www.gamesunique.com**

J. Crew **www.jcrew.com**

Keynote Systems **www.keynote.com**

Kozmo.com **www.kozmo.com**

Proflowers.com **www.proflowers.com**

Reel.com **www.reel.com**

TRUSTe **www.truste.org**

Webvan Group **www.webvan.com**

ZDNet **www.zdnet.com**

Chapter 8

Tracking Visitors and Customers

One big advantage of using the Internet for selling is that you can track almost everything about *how* customers buy your products. Unlike a real-world store, where you get information mostly from sales reports and by observing your shoppers, the Internet provides you with a wealth of information about the shoppers who visit you online.

Web servers can generate site logs, a type of data file that is updated every time someone enters a site. By recording all the traffic and how it moves, these logs can tell you which pages people are visiting, how long they stay there, and how they got there, among other things. Corinne Moore constantly reviews the site logs for Chocoholic.com, a gourmet chocolate retailer in Redwood City, Calif. She believes it's the company's best means for understanding which affiliates and marketing programs are working.

"As we implement special promotions with some of our chocolatiers' products," she says, "we need to give them tangible information about the exposure they are getting, as well as the sales, which they can track. We have been able to refine our affiliate programs based on the data from the site logs to dramatically increase both exposure and sales."

Site logs and tracking software. The Web server that hosts your Web site can track exactly which pages are visited and which buttons or icons are clicked. Site-tracking software can tell you which pages get accessed more than others, which pages bring shoppers forward to another page and which pages make shoppers stop shopping and leave.

TIP In the world of e-commerce, the term "affiliate programs" refers to companies that link Web sites together in order to engage in cooperative sales and/or marketing efforts.

By properly analyzing this data, you can identify the patterns your shoppers tend to follow and change your site to maximize potential business.

If you decide to outsource your Web-site development and hosting, site-tracking software is generally included in your package. If you are unsure of how to analyze the reports you get from your hosting firm, ask them to show you. Most companies will walk you through the information. In fact, you should find out up front if this service is available to you. If you host your own site, there are several site-tracking tools and techniques you can use. Many are free, such as FreeStats or GoldStats by Mediaservices Networks.

To the right is a sample server log. Depending on your service provider and the software you use, the items logged and the terms used to describe them may differ. In this example, *cache* (pronounced "cash") refers to the number of files stored in the user's memory buffer. KB refers to the number of kilobytes of information that are transferred. These items might not be of the utmost importance, but the number of user sessions—3,043 in this example—is very important.

Analyzing your server logs will help you gauge your site's performance

TIP Don't be misled by the number of "hits" reported. Hits do not equal visitors or individual click-throughs! The number of hits is actually determined by the number of individual files called up when someone visits a page on a Web site. If your home page has text, four graphics, and a scrolling marquee, it will register at least six hits every time someone views the page. Set the tracking software to record more useful statistics, such as page views. And make sure you understand the reports your hosting firm supplies.

Tracking

and will alert you to potential problems, as well. For example, under "other response codes," "partial content" may indicate that people have abandoned the site. You could check that Web page and see if it takes a particularly long time to load. "Not found" may mean you have links to other sites or pages that no longer exist. Update the code as necessary. A lot of information is available to give you a picture of activity on your site.

Where do your customers come from? Site tracking will also help you to identify some basic demographic information about your shoppers.

SAMPLE SERVER LOG

Full Statistics for October 2000

Monthly Summary		
Total hits (any request)	100.00%	25493
Total files sent (Code 200)	89.38%	22785
Total files saved by cache (Code 304)	9.62%	2452
Other response codes (see below)	1.00%	256
Total pageviews	9.62%	2452
Remaining responses	90.38%	23041
Total KB requested	100.00%	343495
Total KB transferred (Code 200)	90.56%	311078
Total KB saved by cache (Code 304)	9.44%	32417
Total unique URLs		235
Total unique sites		1905
Total user sessions		3043
Total unique agents		332
Total unique referrer URLs		398

	Maximum	Average
Hits per day	1245	16
Files sent per day	1109	14
Files cached per day	174	1
Pageviews per day	161	1
Sessions per day	166	1
KB sent per day	16898	202

Logfile statistics	
Total logfile entries read	25497
Total logfile entries processed	25493
Empty Request Method	4

Other Response Codes	
Partial Content (Code 206)	100
Moved Permanently (Code 301)	3
Not Found (Code 404)	104
Method Not Allowed (Code 405)	3

Request Methods other than GET/POST	
HEAD	46

Source: Andiron Technologies

Registration forms and cookies will give you more details, but a great deal of general information is available from the tracking software. You will see where your customers are coming from, such as a certain search engine or another site that has a link to your home page. You can tell which domain

SAMPLE LOG REPORT

This page shows how people got to your site. *Referring URL* is what a customer was looking at immediately before coming to your site. Usually there will be a link to your site there, but they could also have selected a bookmarked page or typed in a URL. *Visits* is the number of hits on all of your pages from each source. *Orders* and *Income* shows the sales attributable to each source.

Visits	Orders	Income	Income per Visit	Referring URL
81,850	741	35020.44	0.43	http://altavista.digital.com/ (Many pages) [details]
61,570	76	4351.78	0.07	http://st1.yahoo.com/ (Many pages) [details]
37,724	54	3012.20	0.08	http://store.yahoo.com/ (Many pages) [details]
22,011	389	13618.19	0.62	http://www.msn.com/ (Many pages) [details]
18,261	484	21102.88	1.16	http://search.shopping.yahoo.com/ (Many pages) [details]
11,195	72	3046.24	0.27	http://www.lycos.com/ (Many pages) [details]
10,618	92	4484.05	0.42	http://www.excite.com/ (Many pages) [details]
8,933				http://st1.yahoo.net/ (Many pages) [details]
7,710	107	3198.63	0.41	http://www.looksmart.com/ (Many pages) [details]
5,940	117	6248.45	1.05	http://www.valuenutrition.com/ (Many pages) [details]
5,062	80	3335.60	0.66	http://search.msn.com/ (Many pages) [details]
5,055	60	2570.50	0.51	http://www.infoseek.com/ (Many pages) [details]
4,669	111	4747.97	1.02	http://www.yahoo.com/ (Many pages) [details]
4,599	31	1566.82	0.34	http://stores.yahoo.com/ (Many pages) [details]
4,478	4	276.22	0.06	http://www.viarnall.com/ (Many pages) [details]
3,058	85	5255.70	1.72	http://www.healthstyle.com/ (Many pages) [details]
2,969	27	1017.20	0.34	http://hotbot.lycos.com/ (Many pages) [details]
2,885	52	2422.44	0.84	http://www.google.com/ (Many pages) [details]
2,855	28	1356.75	0.48	http://www.askjeeves.com/ (Many pages) [details]
2,745	27	1000.79	0.36	http://www.ask.com/ (Many pages) [details]
2,446	39	1600.69	0.65	http://www.dogpile.com/ (Many pages) [details]
2,425	58	2295.03	0.95	http://www.infoseek.com/ (Many pages) [details]
2,312	29	977.43	0.42	http://search.metacrawler.com/ (Many pages) [details]
2,168	26	1327.06	0.61	http://google.netscape.com/ (Many pages) [details]
1,976	30	1317.05	0.67	http://www.valuenut.com/ (Many pages) [details]
59,168	8,841	478396.37	8.09	Total not shown
374,682	11,660	603546.53	1.61	**(Total)**

Show

Sort	Period	
○ By Visits	○ Last 10 Days	○ October 1999
○ By Orders	○ Last 30 Days	○ November 1999
○ By Income	○ Last 60 Days	○ December 1999
	○ Last 90 Days	○ January 2000
	○ Last 120 Days	○ February 2000
	● Last 180 Days	

Source: Yahoo! Store

or network is the shopper's host. For example, you can establish how many of your shoppers are AOL members. You can also find out which countries your visitors are logging in from. You might even identify where your shoppers work if they use a company computer. This information can tell you where to spend your advertising dollars and which partnerships you should consider forming.

More details. Depending on their level of sophistication, your site-tracking software and log reports can follow a number of factors and give you a full picture of how well your site works. The example shown on the left, from Yahoo! Store, reveals not only the number of visitors, but also where they came from, how many orders they placed, and the resulting income.

Registration. In addition to receiving passive information from your logs, you can actively gather data from your customers, which will help you to refine your marketing efforts even further. The best tools for this job are registration forms and questionnaires.

When you ask your customers for personal information, it is essential to let them know what you are going to do with it. If you make it clear that you will not sell their records to

TIP Many of these advanced tracking packages work best if they are incorporated into the design up front. So consider the level of tracking you will need in the early stages of your site's production.

any outside lists or services, they will be more inclined to answer your questions. If you can get more details, your market-research efforts will move to the next level, where you can tie the demographic data to your sales reports.

An incentive can be valuable when you ask for more detailed information. After all, you are taking up a customer's time. Consider offering an online coupon or giving the customer access to a special part of the site. Be warned, however, that registration forms placed at the beginning of the shopping path may result in turning off visitors before they even start to shop. In most cases, you will want to wait to ask for registration until the customer is well into the purchase process or even just after it. Keep required information to a minimum. Some sites, such as drugstore.com, have integrated the registration form with the purchase order so that customers are automatically registered the first time they buy something. This can save your shoppers an extra step and give you information you need at the same time.

It's important to figure out how the information will be used before you go live with your questionnaire. Make sure you get the data in a usable report or in a flat file you can import into a spreadsheet or database to fit your needs.

Andiron Technologies offered to anyone who filled out its questionnaire a free video about how to make a fireplace burn cleaner. Everyone at Andiron was delighted with the response, until they realized they had made the mistake of having customers send their information via e-mail. This meant that there was no way to get to the individual answers and sort them. If the answers had been captured in a flat file, Andiron could have easily imported them into its database and made shipping labels and other individualized customer communications. In e-mail form, the answers were just a lot of words that could be made useful only if the company spent the money and effort to re-enter the information into a database.

Tracking advertising activity. The number of people who respond to your banner ads on other sites is easy to track on the Internet. If you have purchased advertising space on someone else's site, that site will provide you with statistics commonly called the "click-through" rate. This shows how many people clicked on your banner ad and went to your site. It is usually presented as a percentage of the number of impressions, or "eyeballs," that saw your ad. You should be able to compare the click-through number supplied to you by the other site against the number of visitors from that site's URL on your referral site logs.

If you offer advertising on your site, you will need tracking software so that, just like television's Nielsen ratings, you can show your advertisers information about their potential audience. To explore your options for selling or trading banners, do a search on your favorite search engine for "banner tracking" or "banner advertising." Many free resources can help you decide how to approach this.

Patterns and trends. It is important to analyze the patterns and trends that develop on your Web site. Do people gravitate to a certain page? Do they buy items on that page? You can capitalize on the popularity of certain items and feature them on your home page. Are entire sections of the site never accessed? Check your navigation. Maybe it's too hard for shoppers to find those sections. Do you find that most shoppers access a similar number of pages? Is there a way to comfortably fit additional products on each page so that the shopper can see more in fewer clicks? Are people going to a certain page but not buying anything? Check out the images and text for the items on that page.

If shoppers are finding the pages but not shopping, there might be something unclear or off-putting about the item description. Perhaps there is a problem with your shopping cart, and they can't figure out how to buy what they want. Which searches do shoppers engage in? You can even track the words people use most often when they search your site. Review the requested terms and queries. They'll give you a bird's-eye view into the minds of your visitors. Are they looking for something you don't carry? Should you carry it? Look at the demographic of your shoppers versus your buyers. What can you learn from that? Should you change your advertising? Analyzing the data collected by your Web site will aid you in refining and improving the e-commerce functions of your Web-based business.

Be proactive. If you take the time to analyze them regularly, server logs and other reports about your site can be powerful forecasting tools—early indicators of demand for your products and the associated backup. When your e-commerce Web site first goes live, you can only estimate the demand for certain items, the quantity and complexity of customer inquiries, and the need for other service functions. Once you're up and running, you will have real feedback, not estimates. These will help you, for instance, to place additional customer-service reps at identified peak times or to have enough inventory, supplies, and shipping personnel ready to spring into action. ■

COMPANIES AND SITES IN THIS CHAPTER

Andiron Technologies **www.ecofire.com**
Chocoholic.com **www.chocoholic.com**
drugstore.com **www.drugstore.com**
FreeStats **www.freestats.com**
GoldStats **www.goldstats.com**

Chapter 9

Evaluations Before and After Launch

The hard decisions have been made. You've decided what information your Web site will include, which features it will have, and how you will handle the technical elements. You've done the research and designed the site that will be your online store to the world. You are *almost* ready to start selling. There are still a few things to do before you "go live."

Testing. Lingerie and apparel seller Victoria's Secret decided to publicize a new line with an online fashion show, which was advertised during the Super Bowl. Thousands of fans turned away from the football game to check out the lingerie models. As you may have read, the overloaded site went down. Unfortunately, the company had forgotten to test the load factor (how many people or transactions can be done simultaneously). Or perhaps they performed the test using faulty audience estimates.

It is *imperative* that you test your site before you go live on the Internet. Tests of your site fall into two general categories. The first is usability testing, which checks whether your site is easy to use and how it looks. The second is technical testing, which ensures that the internal mechanics of the site work properly. Testing the load factor is part of technical testing and is usually accomplished using software that mimics thousands of requests for information from your site. If a reputable developer creates your Web store, he or she will test the site for both usability and technical matters.

Usability testing. Usability testing deals with the appearance, load time, and ease of navigation through your site.This round should include some focus-group testing. A focus group doesn't have to be a formal affair put together by a marketing company, however. The sample doesn't have to be large, but it should cover a range of attitudes and, even more important, a variety of systems. Make sure to test your site on both PCs and Macintoshes, on a variety of processor and modem speeds, on different sizes and brands of monitors, and (if any of your material is to be printed out) on all major brands of printers. Knowing a little HTML code can help if you are attempting to create the site yourself with a WYSIWYG tool. The page you create in Microsoft FrontPage, which looks perfect on the hard drive of your computer, may be skewed when viewed in a browser. If possible, have your evaluators fill out a form recording the type of configuration they used, along with the results.

Evaluation worksheet. To help review other sites as well as your own, dowload the evaluation worksheet from *Inc.* magazine's Web site: www.inc.com/freetools/1,7182,CHL9,00.html. Search the "Free Tool" listing for "Web Site Evaluation Worksheet." The worksheet asks you to assign numerical ratings to a list of e-commerce features and functions. From these ratings, you can determine an overall effectiveness rating for your site or the site you are evaluating.

Technical testing. Your testers should go through the complete purchasing process. Have them fill out your forms, go through the order-taking system, check the tracking, and test any other feature with which your customers

TIP Usability testing includes testing how your site appears, using different browsers and modem speeds. You should view the site through the two main browsers in use today—Netscape Navigator and Microsoft Internet Explorer, which make up 90% of the browser market. Because of the way HTML works, pages are interpreted differently by dissimilar setups. Look at your site on the latest version of these browsers, as well as on older versions. Many of your potential customers may use older computers with small screens and may not have the latest software.

will interact. Below are some of the technical functions you should test:

- *Order processing.* Your order-taking system should be easy and seamless. You want to make sure the instructions to the shopper are clearly written and cover all available options. What happens if a person takes more than a minute or two to enter a credit-card number? What if a customer starts entering a credit-card number and then wants to back out and use a different card? Make sure your order-process system can handle simultaneous transactions.

- *Legacy systems.* If you are linking to your legacy systems—existing hardware and software you use to run your business—check all possible combinations of system interactions.

- *Banking.* Test the transaction throughput to your bank. If electronic deposits are supposed to be completed within 24 hours, make sure they are. Can a fraudulent card get by? Does a valid transaction trigger proper notification? It is much easier to make changes to the site or switch banks or vendors before you go live.

- *E-mail.* If you have decided to use e-mail notification or automatic-reply systems, test them thoroughly, including checking all feedback forms, order confirmations, and requests for information.

- *Tracking.* Test your tracking and reporting software. Be sure your software provides the expected data and feedback.

- *Load testing.* As illustrated by the Victoria's Secret story, it's essential to make sure your site can handle a large amount of traffic. Programs are available to help you simulate huge numbers of simultaneous requests for the site.

- *Business responsibilities.* If you want visitors, customers, and sales, it's your responsibility to be sure your Web site operates as smoothly as possible. In addition, you have other business responsibilities. Just because you are selling in cyberspace doesn't mean you can ignore legal issues and local requirements. The following are a few questions you should address:

- Does your city or town require a business license?
- What are the legal requirements for keeping records and data?
- Are your back-up procedures working?
- Have you obtained a federal ID number and filed with your state franchise tax board?
- Have you secured the appropriate business insurance?

Best practices in e-commerce security. If you conduct e-commerce, you need to have order information and any sensitive transactions conducted on secure servers that encrypt the information. Any server connected to the Internet for e-commerce should sit behind a firewall—a combination of special hardware and software that acts as a barrier between your company's computers and the Internet. It allows information to be received, but protects your system from intruders. And remember, firewalls and server software need to be kept up to date.

TIP Security is physical as well as electronic. Don't forget to enforce commonsense, real-world security. Don't keep passwords in plain sight. Don't include customer credit-card numbers on widely distributed reports. Keep confidential information as secure in the physical world as in the electronic one.

Another security precaution is data backup. Perform backups once a day or more, and consider keeping a duplicate at another location.

Security is not a simple issue. There is a lot to know about computers and security—in itself a good reason to outsource your hosting to an established hosting firm. Find out what your hosting firm's security practices are. Talk to your hosting provider, as well as to software and security consultants, if you keep any of the hosting in-house.

After you're up and running. At some

point, you'll feel comfortable with your site and you'll "open your doors" for business. But the evaluation process should not stop. Here are some "big picture" items that should let you know whether your site is turning into a winner or a loser.

How do you know that you're winning?
- You can't keep up with orders.
- You're getting more visitors per day than you'd ever imagined.
- You've exceeded your bandwidth.
- You've run out of inventory.
- You're reading compliments about your site in newsgroups.

(Note: These positive indicators can quickly become problems if they aren't addressed.)

How do you know that you're losing?
- You have no traffic to speak of.
- You have no orders.
- You aren't visible in search engines.
- You're getting customer complaints.
- Your site fails during transaction load.
- You're reading complaints about your site in newsgroups.

Success and failure. As with any new venture, it is important to establish clear goals so that you can measure your success. If you're getting a lot of page views, you know your marketing is working. Using more bandwidth than you expected is another sign of success. Of course, the number of orders is the best way to judge your online performance.

On the other hand, these statistics can be an early indicator of potential failure. If you aren't getting traffic to your Web site, your marketing campaign isn't working. Make sure to check the tags (keywords) that identify your site so that the search engines bring up your site when people look for your type of product or service. If you are getting lots of traffic but making few sales, your marketing is fine but something may be off with your site design or the product itself. Determine at which point shoppers leave your site, and search for clues.

Are you receiving complaints? For many people, it's easier to gripe on the Internet than in person. Listen to what your customers are saying, and see if you can change things. In the real world, a shopper may tell 10 people about a negative experience. On the Web, it's just as easy to tell 10,000.

Is it worth it? When your site was just brochureware, it might have been difficult to determine the effectiveness of your efforts. When you sell on the Web, there's enough data available to get a good handle on what's happening. Your ROI equals the net income divided by assets. To determine your benefits, you need records of what it cost to build, maintain, and support your site. Your cost of sales should be easy to determine.

Don't rush to conclusions if your ROI isn't what you expected in the first few months. You have to find the right marketing, design, and product mix to succeed, so keep refining and testing your site and products. When you find the combination that works, your Web store will be a worthwhile addition to your real-world business.

For a businessperson, e-commerce is no longer an alternative sales channel. It's becoming an imperative! It's a whole new way of thinking and doing business. E-commerce is about expanding into new markets and sales channels. It's about improved service for your customers and efficient business systems for your company. Now is the time to start building your business into an e-commerce-enabled venture. ∎

COMPANIES AND SITES IN THIS CHAPTER

Victoria's Secret
www.victoriassecret.com
Microsoft **www.microsoft.com**

• CyberSpeak •

Application service provider (ASP) A third-party entity that manages and leases software-based services and solutions to customers across the Internet from a central data center. ASPs provide a way for companies to outsource some or all aspects of their information technology needs.

Bandwidth The capacity of the transmission of information (text, images, video, sound) that can be sent through an Internet connection.

Banner ad A graphic image on a Web page used for advertising, which is linked to the advertiser's Web site.

Beta site A version of a Web site that is very close to the final version, but not yet live, which is tested under real conditions.

Bricks and mortar A physical location as opposed to a "virtual" online presence.

Brochureware site A noninteractive, static Web site that portrays information about a company in a manner similar to a print brochure.

Clicks and mortar A business model in which companies combine real-world business with e-commerce.

Click-through rate The percentage of users who have viewed a banner ad and then clicked on it to access the advertised Web site.

Commerce service provider (CSP) A third-party entity similar to an ASP, which manages and distributes software-based e-commerce services and solutions to customers via the Internet.

Cookies Small files created by a Web server and stored on the user's hard drive. They allow the Web server to recognize visitors and track and display users' patterns.

Domain The address of a Web site that identifies its location. For example, http://www.inc.com is the domain of *Inc.* magazine.

Electronic-business service provider (EBSP) A third-party entity similar to an ASP and CSP, which manages and distributes software-based services and solutions across the Internet. EBSPs offer common business services, such as payroll processing, in addition to e-commerce services.

Firewall A security barrier placed between a company's internal computer network and the Internet. Designed to keep private information in and intruders out.

• CyberSpeak •

Flat file A file that contains data fields such as customer's last name and first name, city and state, each separated by a "delimiter," such as a comma or tab. This type of file can be imported into database and spreadsheet programs.

Frequently asked questions (FAQs) A group of questions about a subject, which visitors have asked repeatedly, along with the answers.

Freeware Software that can be downloaded from the Internet without cost. Also known as shareware.

Gateway A combination of hardware and software that translates data so that it can be accessed and understood by two or more sets of computers linked by the gateway. One example is a payment gateway.

Hit The number of times a file on a Web page is requested by a browser.

Host The computer from which the files that constitute a Web site are delivered and maintained.

Hypertext markup language (HTML) A text-based language used in the construction of Web pages that is interpreted by Web browsers.

Hypertext link A word or group of words in the text of a Web site, which are visually highlighted. When the user clicks on the hypertext link, he or she is transported to a different URL or to another location on the same Web site, depending on the nature of the link.

Internet The world's largest computer network, consisting of private, commercial, educational, and government computers linked by telephone, cable TV, fiber-optic lines, and microwave and satellite signals.

Internet service provider (ISP) A company that provides access to the Internet through dial-up or high-speed connections. Many ISPs have transformed themselves into CSPs by offering additional, related services.

Intranet A private network, usually maintained by a mid- or large-sized company for internal communications. Intranets use the same communications protocols and hypertext links as the Web and thus provide a standard way of disseminating information.

Legacy system The existing hardware and software a company uses to run its business.

Navigation bar A set of buttons, words, or graphic images, typically in a row or column, used as a resource that links to major topic sections on a Web site.

Page view A measurement of how often a page is seen by users. A page view is the first viewing of one complete HTML file by each browser.

Search engine An online software application used to locate information and Web sites.

Secure hypertext transfer protocol (S-HTTP) An extension to the HTTP protocol to support secure data transmission over the Web. Another technology for transmitting secure communications over the Web is secure sockets layer, (SSL) below, which is more prevalent.

Secure sockets layer (SSL) A protocol developed by Netscape for transmitting private documents via the Internet. SSL works by using a private-key technology to encrypt data that is transferred over the SSL connection. Major browsers support SSL, and many Web sites use the protocol to obtain confidential user information, such as credit-card numbers.

Server log A file on a Web server that is updated every time a site is accessed. The server log records information, including IP address, dates and times, and other information about the traffic.

Shopping cart Software that enables an online store's ordering process. Typically, a shopping cart is the interface between a company's Web site and its deeper infrastructure, allowing consumers to select merchandise, review what they have selected, make necessary modifications or additions, and purchase the merchandise.

Uniform resource locator (URL) The global address of documents and other resources on the World Wide Web. URLs are typed into the browser to access Web pages, and they are embedded in the pages themselves to provide hypertext links to other pages.

Web server A computer that is linked by communication lines to the Internet and serves up information in the form of text, graphics, and multimedia. Any computer can be turned into a Web server by installing server software and connecting it to the Internet.

WYSIWYG An application that displays on the screen exactly what will appear when the document is printed. The acronym is pronounced "wizzy-wig" and stands for "what you see is what you get." ■

About the Authors

Loël McPhee is a consultant for e-commerce enterprises worldwide. She was formerly director of strategic partnerships and research for CommerceNet, a global consortium of more than 600 e-commerce companies. While at CommerceNet, McPhee led the *Demographics of the Internet* studies, conducted with Nielsen Media Research. She also created CommerceNet Press, producing a series of e-commerce books to educate the business community. A successful entrepreneur, McPhee has five start-ups to her credit, most recently cofounding Andiron Technologies, an environmental-solutions product development company. She can be contacted at loel@andirontechnologies.com.

Peri Drucker is Global Manager, Industries, at Entrust Technologies, a global leader in PKI (public key infrastructure) and Internet security. Previously, Drucker directed the marketing activities of CommerceNet, the e-commerce consortium. Before that she was project director at Bay Area Multimedia Partnership, where she developed SkillsNet, a workforce development initiative for the multimedia and digital entertainment industries. Drucker is also coauthor of *A Labor Market Analysis: Opportunities in Multimedia*. Her e-mail address is perid@mail.com.

Robert Cormia is an Internet technologist and e-business consultant. Cormia, who began working with the Internet in 1994, developed the e-commerce curriculum at Foothill College while working as a market analyst for G2R, a market research firm, where he specialized in IT strategy development for *Fortune* 500 enterprises. In 1998, he joined eCongo.com, a provider of free e-commerce services, as corporate strategist and product developer. Cormia joined Calkey.com in March 2000, as an adviser in training and education development for UML (unified modeling language) users. He can be contacted at rdcormia@best.com.

Cathy Hammer designs, produces, and facilitates educational programs that emphasize workflow and performance improvement. She has led seminars and computer-based projects for entrepreneurs and large organizations. Recently, Hammer has focused on fostering knowledge and alignment among technical and creative departments. Her latest venture is NetSavvy Training, a series of workshops providing non-technical personnel with a basic understanding of the Internet. She can be reached at chammer@netsavvytraining.com. ■